WALKS IN DALES COUNTRY

an illustrated guide to
thirty scenic walks

by

J. Keighley

CICERONE PRESS
MILNTHORPE CUMBRIA
www.cicerone.co.uk

Reprinted 2002, 2009
ISBN-13: 978 1 85284 323 6
ISBN-10: 1 85284 323 3

Also by *JKeighley*

WALKS IN THE YORKSHIRE DALES
ISBN 1 85284 034 X

WALKS IN THE YORKSHIRE DALES – BOOK TWO
ISBN 1 85284 065 X

WALKS IN THE YORKSHIRE DALES – BOOK THREE
ISBN 1 85284 085 4

WALKS IN LANCASHIRE WITCH COUNTRY
ISBN 1 85284 093 5

WALKS ON THE NORTH YORK MOORS
ISBN 1 85284 134 6

WALKS ON THE NORTH YORK MOORS – BOOK TWO
ISBN 1 85284 197 4

FAMILY WALKS IN THE FOREST OF BOWLAND
ISBN 1 85284 251 2

WALKS IN RIBBLE COUNTRY
ISBN 1 85284 284 9

INTRODUCTION

The area known as the Yorkshire Dales is many things to many people, but above all it is magnificent walking country. Walking has traditionally been the favourite pursuit of those visiting a region which offers a range of attractions perhaps unrivalled anywhere else in the whole of Britain :-

- wild, desolate fells
- extensive tracts of heather moorland
- rugged limestone scars, pavements and spectacular cliffs
- awe-inspiring potholes and caves
- deep river gorges and sparkling mountain streams
- exquisitely beautiful waterfalls
- green fertile valleys and flowery meadows
- outstanding views
- a vast network of public footpaths and bridleways
- remote, picturesque villages and bustling market towns
- ancient abbeys, churches and castles
- fascinating relics of former industries and ancient civilizations

The happiest person in the Dales must be the walker who is also a geologist. The major part of the area lies on a platform of ancient rock – chiefly granite – known as the Askrigg Block. Apart from a few isolated exceptions, however, this base platform lies covered by strata of more recently formed rocks, and of these it is limestone which dominates the geology, and consequently the scenery, of the Yorkshire Dales.

The Great Scar Limestone is up to 400 feet thick in parts of the western and southern Dales, and is magnificently exposed in Ribblesdale, Wharfedale and Malhamdale. Here, above the glistening cliffs and scars, are vast areas of limestone pavements weathered from the exposed blocks of rocks. About half the limestone pavement in Britain is found in the Yorkshire Dales. The Great Scar Limestone has not only undergone surface erosion, but is also honeycombed with complex underground cave systems. This is probably the finest caving area in Britain. The ordinary walker, who is too faint-hearted (or sensible?) to venture into these dank and sinister caverns, can safely sample the wonders of the underworld at three public show caves – White Scar Cave (Ingleton), Ingleborough Cave (Clapham) and Stump Cross Caverns (between Pateley Bridge and Grassington).

In the more northerly dales, notably Wensleydale and Swaledale, the Great Scar Limestone lies hidden beneath layers of rock strata known as the Yordale Series. Formed in an alternate succession of sandstone, shale and limestone (of a darker kind than the Great Scar variety), the Yoredales have weathered to produce hillsides with a distinctive stepped profile. In all parts of the Dales the highest fells are capped by beds of hard, coarse millstone grit.

5

Though nature has lavishly contributed this fine scenery, it is the influence of man which has helped to create the unique Dales landscape that we see today. The mineral resources of the region have been exploited for many centuries. The Romans are known to have mined lead, and this industry developed until, at its peak in the nineteenth century, thousands of miners, chiefly in Swaledale and Wharfedale, were employed in extracting and processing lead. The ruins, levels, hushes and spoil heaps of these old mines still remain — stark and grim and desolate.

Since the discovery that grassland was improved by the application of burnt limestone (hence the profusion of old lime kilns), limestone working has developed into a major Dales industry, and today high-quality limestone is quarried in several areas — most notably at Cracoe and Horton-in-Ribblesdale.

In the eighteenth century certain changes in the country's social and economic life had a marked effect on the Dales landscape. Between 1780 and 1820 successive Enclosure Acts led to a re-distribution of land and the construction of thousands of miles of drystone walls in the valleys and up the fellsides. This was an important building period in the Dales, and many of the present farms, cottages and barns are of that vintage. The Dales in fact have been inhabited since pre-history, and current walkers' paths date from earliest man to the drovers' and packhorse routes of the last two or three centuries. Many of these ancient green lanes still provide superb routes over the hills from dale to dale.

The other great influence on the landscape has been the grazing of sheep. The Dales are renowned for sheep, and years of careful breeding has produced animals which are ideally suited to the terrain and climate. Most popular is the famous blackfaced 'Swaledale' with its curly horns. The Yorkshire Dales National Park Authority has chosen the Swaledale tup as its symbol. Sheep-grazing has a profound effect on the natural vegetation of the area.

My purpose in writing this introduction has been to attempt a general description of the superb countryside which the lucky user of this book may expect to enjoy, and the major factors which have shaped and fashioned it. My sincere wish is that you may derive as much pleasure from these walks as I have had in compiling them.

J Keighley

Skipton   August 2000

ABOUT THIS BOOK

THE WALKS

All the walks described in this book are circular, and begin at a place where a car may be parked without causing an obstruction. They are fairly uniform in length, an average of just over 6 miles making them half-day rather than full-day excursions. The routes, which adhere to public rights-of-way and permissive paths, should be free from serious difficulty and well within the capability of reasonably fit and agile walkers. Although the author has personally researched and walked all these routes, it must be pointed out that changes will occur quite frequently. Walkers may expect to encounter new stiles and fences and even diversions – either temporary or permanent. In such cases please note and obey all legitimate waymarks and signs.

NEITHER THE AUTHOR NOR THE PUBLISHER CAN ACCEPT RESPONSIBILITY FOR ANY ACCIDENT OR MISADVENTURE INCURRED ON THESE WALKS.

THE MAPS

The strip-maps show all relevant route-finding features, and great care has been taken to ensure accuracy, although for the sake of clarity there is deliberate distortion of scale in depicting routes along, for example, narrow lanes or through farmyards. In all maps north is at the top. In the Route Directions any mention of a stile, gate or footbridge means that it is used, unless otherwise stated. The maps and route directions together should suffice to make it quite clear to you how you've got lost. It is, however, strongly recommended that an Ordnance Survey map be carried, as this will add interest and enable the walker to identify distant features not mentioned in the text. A full list of the Ordnance Survey maps needed to cover the area can be found on Page 11.

SYMBOLS USED ON THE MAPS

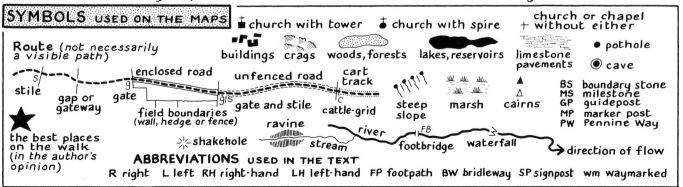

Route (not necessarily a visible path)
stile
gap or gateway
gate
enclosed road
field boundaries (wall, hedge or fence)
gate and stile
unfenced road
cart track
cattle-grid
the best places on the walk (in the author's opinion)
shakehole
ravine
stream
steep slope
marsh
cairns
river
footbridge
waterfall
direction of flow

🏰 church with tower   ♱ church with spire   + church or chapel without either

buildings   crags   woods, forests   lakes, reservoirs   limestone pavements

● pothole
◉ cave

BS boundary stone
MS milestone
GP guidepost
MP marker post
PW Pennine Way

ABBREVIATIONS USED IN THE TEXT
R right   L left   RH right-hand   LH left-hand   FP footpath   BW bridleway   SP signpost   wm waymarked

WALKING IN THE DALES

✳ Many of the routes in this book cross agricultural land, and farmers will not welcome incon-siderate visitors. When crossing fields keep closely to paths and walk in single file across meadows. Avoid climbing walls, and securely close all gates behind you (unless they are obviously meant to be left open).

✳ Cars must not be parked where they obstruct field gates or cause damage to grass verges. Lock your car and hide from view any attractive or valuable articles (or take them with you).

✳ Some of the walks described in this book cross high, exposed moorland terrain where the weather conditions may be less pleasant than at valley level. Should the weather turn nasty, don't hesitate to call it a day and return by the route along which you came.

✳ Before setting out, let others know exactly where you're going (especially if you're walking alone).

✳ When walking along a motor-road walk on the RIGHT to face oncoming traffic. The exception to this is on approaching a blind right-hand bend, when you should cross to the left for a clearer view.

CLOTHING AND EQUIPMENT

Boots or strong, comfortable shoes are essential (on the high moors and in winter BOOTS are the ONLY suitable footwear). A windproof jacket (preferably with a hood) will be needed. Thick, heavy sweaters are not a good idea - two or three lightweight layers are warmer and more adaptable to changing conditions. Denim is not at all suitable. In cold weather a woollen hat or cap will prevent the loss of a great deal of body heat. A rucksack is necessary. A small 'daysack' with a capacity of about 20-25 litres would be adequate for any of these walks. The author's rucksack will always contain the following items :-

● waterproof jacket and overtrousers ● small first aid kit ● spare laces ● large-scale O.S. map ● compass ● whistle ● plastic bottle for cold drink and/or flask for coffee or soup ● a high-calorie snack (e.g. chocolate or crisps) ● dog's drinking-water in a plastic bottle with either a 'cup-top' or a separate small bowl.

In wet, muddy conditions gaiters are an asset, once you've managed to get them on (it helps if you're a contortionist). A walking-stick is a matter of personal preference. Some walkers wouldn't be seen dead with one, but the author finds a knobstick useful for steep, slippery descents, fording streams, beating down nettles, discouraging aggressive animals and testing potentially boggy ground prior to sinking in up to the knees. Folding, or telescopic, metal jobs which are stuffable into a rucksack are now popular (though pricey)

CHILDREN When taking children on country walks some thought must be given to distance and the type of terrain involved. Until you're sure of the child's capabilities, keep the distance short. Most of the walks in this book would probably be too much for a child under the age of five. As a rough rule-of-thumb, a child should be able to manage about a mile for each year of his age after his fifth birthday. Children should be warmly clothed and well shod. One cannot always afford to buy expensive boots for growing feet, but at least the child should have strong shoes or close-fitting wellies. On no account should young children be allowed to wander off beyond the range of vision of responsible adults, and extreme care and control must be exercised in the vicinity of crags, quarries, potholes, old mine workings and ruined buildings.

DOGS Though dogs are generally better-behaved than children they can nevertheless present certain difficulties which the owner should bear in mind. The two main problems are livestock and stiles - particularly ladder-stiles. Dogs should be kept under close control at all times, and MUST be on a lead in the proximity of farmyards and farm livestock. You will be lucky to complete any of these walks without encountering cattle and/or sheep. A lead should also be used when walking on motor-roads or on moorland during nesting-time (April-June). Some large, agile dogs are able to scramble over ladder-stiles, but small models need to be lifted over, and this can sometimes be rather awkward if you're walking alone. If your dog is big, fat and rheumaticky then you have problems. Best places for dogs are high, open ground and woodland; worst are motor-roads and lowland pastures. On very hot, sunny days dogs can become distressed, and may be at risk of heat-stroke. On summer walks the author has in his rucksack a small, plastic spray-bottle of water.

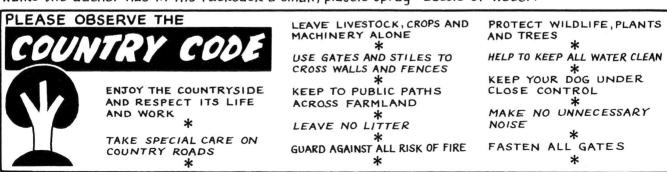

PLEASE OBSERVE THE

COUNTRY CODE

ENJOY THE COUNTRYSIDE AND RESPECT ITS LIFE AND WORK
*
TAKE SPECIAL CARE ON COUNTRY ROADS
*

LEAVE LIVESTOCK, CROPS AND MACHINERY ALONE
*
USE GATES AND STILES TO CROSS WALLS AND FENCES
*
KEEP TO PUBLIC PATHS ACROSS FARMLAND
*
LEAVE NO LITTER
*
GUARD AGAINST ALL RISK OF FIRE
*

PROTECT WILDLIFE, PLANTS AND TREES
*
HELP TO KEEP ALL WATER CLEAN
*
KEEP YOUR DOG UNDER CLOSE CONTROL
*
MAKE NO UNNECESSARY NOISE
*
FASTEN ALL GATES
*

THE WALKS

• EASY   •• MODERATE   ••• STRENUOUS

No		MILES
1	THE SPLENDOURS OF MALHAM ••	7¾
2	UPPER ARKENGARTHDALE •	6½
3	BLUBBERHOUSES •	5¾
4	DRUMALDRACE ••	5½
5	MARBLE STEPS POT ••	5½
6	AZERLEY PARK •	6
7	DENT AND GAWTHROP ••	5
8	SWINNER GILL AND KISDON •••	8½
9	THE MONK'S ROAD ••	6½
10	LEAD MINES OF NIDDERDALE ••	6½
11	MAIDEN CASTLE ••	4¾
12	LOWER BISHOPDALE •	6½
13	THE XII APOSTLES ••	5
14	JERVAULX ABBEY AND EAST WITTON ••	7½
15	THE HEART OF WHARFEDALE •	6¾
16	THE ASCENT OF LITTLE WHERNSIDE •••	8½
17	HELL GILL •	4¾

No		MILES
18	PINHAW BEACON •••	7½
19	MAJESTIC INGLEBOROUGH •••	8½
20	A CIRCUIT OF THRUSCROSS RESERVOIR •	4¾
21	THREE CRAVEN VILLAGES •	6¼
22	FOUNTAINS ABBEY AND SAWLEY •	5¾
23	SEMERWATER AND THE ROMAN ROAD ••	5½
24	HARE HEAD AND BOLTON PRIORY ••	7½
25	COVERDALE ••	6
26	JOHN O' GAUNT'S CASTLE •	4½
27	BARBONDALE ••	8½
28	AIRTON AND BELL BUSK •	5
29	REDMIRE FORCE AND THE TEMPLARS' CHAPEL •	6¾
30	HORSE HEAD •••	7¾

✸

SEVEN ORDNANCE SURVEY (1:25 000) MAPS WILL BE NEEDED TO COVER ALL THE WALKS IN THIS BOOK.

CODE

A OUTDOOR LEISURE 2 YORKSHIRE DALES Southern and Western areas
B OUTDOOR LEISURE 19 HOWGILL FELLS AND UPPER EDEN VALLEY
C OUTDOOR LEISURE 21 SOUTH PENNINES
D OUTDOOR LEISURE 30 YORKSHIRE DALES Northern and Central areas
E EXPLORER 26 NIDDERDALE
F EXPLORER 27 LOWER WHARFEDALE AND WASHBURN VALLEY
G PATHFINDER 630 (SE 17/18) MIDDLEHAM AND JERVAULX ABBEY

 ✱

NATIONAL PARK CENTRES

AYSGARTH FALLS   (01969) 663424
CLAPHAM   (015242) 51419
GRASSINGTON   (01756) 752774
HAWES   (01969) 667450
MALHAM   (01729) 830363
REETH   (01748) 884059
SEDBERGH   (015396) 20125

OPENING TIMES

APRIL TO OCTOBER, DAILY, 10AM – 5PM

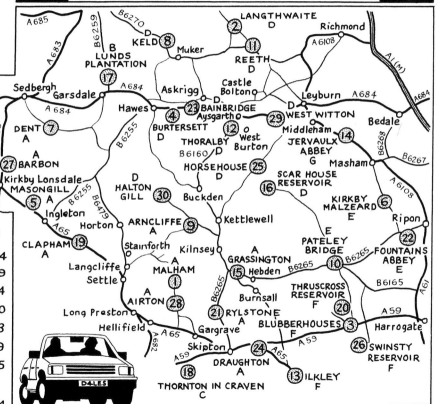

ROAD MAP OF THE AREA
SHOWING THE STARTING POINTS
OF THE 30 WALKS DESCRIBED IN THIS BOOK

1 THE SPLENDOURS OF MALHAM 7¾ MILES

P Malham. Large car park (pay and display) at National Park Centre. Grid ref: 900 626

ROUTE DIRECTIONS

① From National Park Centre cross road to stile (SP Hanlith Bridge 1m). Follow wall on L across two fields. ② In next field small cairns mark route forward to gated step-stile. Continue along obvious path, which eventually passes R of buildings to gate. ③ Fork R off drive up green path to wall-stile. Maintain direction to another wall-stile, then head for barn at very far LH corner. ④ Follow road L through village. Turn L along lane (SP Hanlith ½). Beyond bridge the lane climbs steeply, eventually zig-zagging up to Windy Pike Farm. Continue up walled track to its end at a gate. ⑤ Straight up on broad green path with marker posts. At 4-way SP bear L (BW Weets Top ¼). Keep parallel with wall on L to summit. ⑥ Through gate, down rough track and L down tarmac lane. ⑦ For short detour to Gordale Scar take gate on R (FP Gordale Scar). Return to pass Gordale Bridge and in 100yds take gate on L to visit Janet's Foss. ⑧ Return to bridge and go L through gate (FP Malham Cove). Bear L past wall-corner and up alongside wall. Through gate and up to steps and gate, then go L along 'made' path. ⑨ Cross road to stiles. Forward up cart-track then straight ahead along green path to fingerpost. Bear L down to gateway. ⑩ Cross top of Cove (see NOTE R) to triple stile at far end of limestone pavement. Descend steps and go R along

AVOID MALHAM AT WEEKENDS, UNLESS YOU DON'T MIND QUEUEING AT STILES.

The Cove ⑩
steps
clapper bridge
wall
Malham Beck
⑪
National Park Centre car park and toilets
MALHAM ①
FB
② Gordale Beck
Aire Head Springs
seat
③ Scalegill (former mill)
Out Gang (barn)
ruin
plantation
Windy Pike Farm
④ Hanlith
Hall Hanlith Bridge
KIRKBY MALHAM
R. Aire

Grey Gill ⑨
Cawden Flats Barn
⑧ Janet's Foss ⑦
modern barns
ruin
barn
Gordale Beck
Gordale House
Hawthorns Lane
Gordale Scar ★
Cross Field Knotts ★
⑥ cross O.S. col.
Weets Top 1357 ★
The Weets
Hetton
SP
Hanlith Gill Syke
Calton 2½
⑤
broad path with marker posts
Hanlith Moor
wall

MDCCC XL
sundial, Victoria Inn, Kirkby Malham

NOTE: You are strongly advised to cross the top of The Cove via the raised grassy outcrops to the R of the limestone pavement. Small children and dogs should **ALWAYS** be taken this way. Crossing the pavement demands **CARE** and **CONCENTRATION**, especially in wet weather, and a fall into one of the deep grikes could cause serious injury.

12

■ ■

MALHAM IS ONE OF THE MOST FAMOUS WALKING AREAS IN BRITAIN, AND ITS FAME IS RICHLY DESERVED, FOR ITS SPECTACULAR LIMESTONE SCENERY IS ABSOLUTELY STUNNING – A SUBLIME BLEND OF GREY-WHITE ROCK, LIGHT-GREEN VELVETY TURF AND BLUE SKY (OCCASIONALLY!). STARKLY CONTRASTING ARE THE BLEAK AND SOMBRE GRITSTONE MOORS WHICH LIE TO THE SOUTH OF THE MID-CRAVEN FAULT, AND OVER WHICH OUR WALK BEGINS. THERE IS A CLIMB OF 700' FROM HANLITH BRIDGE TO WEETS TOP – INITIALLY ON STEEP TARMAC BUT WITH GENTLE GRADIENTS BEYOND WINDY PIKE. 2 LADDER-STILES (BOTH WITH ADJACENT STEP-STILES). CLEAR PATHS THROUGHOUT. LESS THAN A MILE ON MOTOR-ROADS.

1

MAP A

gravel path. ⑪▶ Turn L to follow road down to Malham.

☆**MALHAM** has a resident population of only about 130, but its unique attractions mean that it is always thronged with visitors. The village has many ancient and interesting buildings, and its rustic charm is undeniable. An excellent leaflet, 'Malham village walk', obtainable from the National Park Centre, provides a circular walk of less than one hour describing the historical features of this utterly fascinating place.

AIRE HEAD SPRINGS is where a stream from Malham Tarn emerges from a 3-mile subterranean journey.

KIRKBY MALHAM Don't go dashing through this tiny village without paying a visit to its magnificent and venerable (c 1490) church, which is known as the 'Cathedral of the Dales'. Its doors are ever-open to welcome visitors, and a guidebook is available to identify its many interesting features.

Monk Bridge, Malham

Hanlith Bridge

WEETS TOP is the summit of a gritstone hill which, like many another of that ilk, is somewhat drab and soggy. It is, however, one of the finest vantage points in the area. Just through the gate in the wall is the restored **WEETS CROSS**, probably of monastic origin.

GORDALE SCAR – one of the most spectacular landforms in England – is an awe-inspiring gorge with walls towering to a height of 150 feet.

JANET'S FOSS is a pretty waterfall set in the lovely little dell of Gordale Beck. There is an information board nearby.

THE COVE is Malham's N°1 attraction. This dramatic limestone cliff-650' wide and nearly 300' high – is the finest piece of rock scenery in the country. There is a sensational view from the splendid limestone pavement at the top.

THE NATIONAL TRUST
MALHAM COVE FIELDS

13

B
A
Kitley Hill
High Faggergill
⑦
⑥
ruin
⑤
Low Faggergill
barn
wall
fence
Kitley Hill House
wall
Gales Gate
④
wall
fence
boulders
farm road
farm road
WHAW
barn barn
seat
hut
⑧
BW
B
A
tarmac road
Whaw Bridge
gls
wall
Arkle Beck
High Eskeleth
unusual stile
FB
pretty woodland path
Arkle Beck
former chapel
barns
FB
⑨
Powder House
③
⑩
Scar House

Langthwaite village has a friendly feel about it, although the notice on the toilets - WELCOME TO LANGTHWAITE PUBLIC CONVENIENCES - is perhaps a little OTT.

②
chapel (toilets opposite)
①
LANGTHWAITE
car park

ROUTE DIRECTIONS

① From car park walk R along main road. ② Fork R along lane past church. At West House fork L to wall-stile, then turn L and follow farm road. ③ Cross road to gate/stile. Go upstream to cross footbridge, then turn L to stile. Follow obvious riverside path. At hamlet of Whaw keep straight on along beckside lane. ④ Turn L along drive signed 'Low Faggergill'. When it forks keep L. Enter farmyard and keep R of house to ascend farm road. ⑤ From gate in crosswall (where wall on R ends) go forward for about 45yds then turn ½ R onto rough pasture. Very sketchy path - make a beeline for the distant farm. Locate a gated stile in wall on R and climb, via a ladder-stile, to farm. ⑥ Go round to R of buildings, through 2 gates then R and R again along farm road. ⑦ Just before reaching wall on L turn L up green path. Follow wall on R to join descending farm road. ⑧ Turn L along road. ⑨ At T-junction cross to stile (FP Langthwaite 1) and cross field to stile at far LH corner. Continue forward to plank bridge/gate and clear path through wood. ⑩ Emerge from trees to be confronted by two large houses (Scar House on L, Usher Cottage on R). Pass to R of Usher Cottage to gate/stile (wm). Keep straight on along generally clear path to Langthwaite. Turn R through village to main road and car park.

This unusual hexagonal building may be seen from several points on the route. It is a Powder House, built in 1807 to store gunpowder used in the local mines.

LANGTHWAITE CHURCH (1817) is one of many 'Waterloo' churches which were built with money provided by Parliament as a thanksgiving for Wellington's victory over Napoleon (pictured R) at the Battle of Waterloo (18-6-1815).

EASY WALKING THROUGH RIVERSIDE MEADOWS AND ALONG FARM TRACKS AND QUIET LANES. THOUGH MOSTLY SET AMID THE SYLVAN SCENERY OF THE LIVELY ARKLE BECK, THE WALK OFFERS A GLIMPSE OF THE LONELY, BLEAK AND MINE-SCARRED MOORS AT THE NORTHERN EXTREMITY OF THE NATIONAL PARK — AN AREA RARELY VISITED BY WALKERS. ONLY 1 LADDER-STILE. 1¼ MILES ON VIRTUALLY TRAFFIC-FREE MOTOR-ROADS. FROM THE MEMORIAL SEAT AT POINT ⑧ THERE IS AN EXQUISITE VIEW DOWN THE DALE; YOU'D BE HARD-PRESSED TO FIND A LOVELIER PLACE THAN THIS.

2

MAP D

ARKENGARTHDALE

is Yorkshire's most northerly Pennine Dale and the Swale's major tributary valley. The fast-flowing Arkle Beck rises on the bleak moors near the famous Tan Hill Inn (England's highest pub) and flows for 11 miles to join the Swale at Grinton. Arkengarthdale was a busy lead-mining area until about 1890, when cheap imports killed the industry, and for over a century nature has struggled in vain to conceal the ravages of man. Though the valley bottom is delightfully pastoral and well-wooded, the upper fellsides are still slashed by the scars caused by hushing (✱), and barren spoil heaps mark the sites of mine entrances and former crushing plants.

(✱) a system where deliberate flooding of part of a hillside gouged away the top soil to reveal the underlying ore-bearing strata.

LANGTHWAITE

Chapel Farm

The tiny hamlet of **WHAW** used to have two inns. Both are long gone, but there's a nice tea room at Chapel Farm.

High Faggergill

On the bleak moors behind this lonely, windswept farm was Faggergill Mine, one of the largest lead mines in the area.

is the only place in Arkengarthdale that can be called a village. Some of its buildings are scattered alongside the main valley road, but the hub of the village is the attractive cluster of houses huddled around a pub on the E side of the beck. The oak altar in the CHURCH OF ST. MARY THE VIRGIN is the work of Robert Thompson of Kilburn. The mouse trademark of this famous woodcarver can be well seen on the wall plate on the N wall. The churchyard has been used for several films. Emma Harte, 'A Woman of Substance', was 'buried' here in the sequel film 'Hold The Dream'.

✱ Near the end of the walk you will pass the pitch of the ARKENGARTHDALE QUOITS CLUB. Quoits is a very popular game in the Northern Dales. A 2½-3 lb iron ring, or quoit (the old lead-miners used horseshoes) is thrown towards a vertical pin, and a quoit falling over the pin (a 'ringer') scores 2 pts. One landing nearest the pin scores 1 pt. Games are 21-up. The local league has teams (7 players) from Arkengarthdale, Reeth, Low Row, Grinton and Richmond.

3 BLUBBERHOUSES 5¾ MILES

ROUTE DIRECTIONS

P Blubberhouses. Large layby alongside the A59 Harrogate - Skipton road, at the head of Fewston Reservoir and just below the prominent little church. Grid ref : 168 553

① From layby entrance cross main road and walk along Hall Lane (SP West End 2½). ② At RH bend go straight ahead through gate (BW sign) and up cart-track. ③ Cart-track meets tarmac road. FOR SHORT CUT, to avoid rough section on Kex Gill Moor, turn R and follow road directly to point ⑧ (Reduces walk to 4¼ miles). FOR FULL WALK keep straight on for 100yds, then turn L to walk along LH side of wall. When wall ends continue towards quarry buildings. ④ At small plantation turn L alongside fence. At fence-corner keep on down to prominent gritstone outcrop. From just above it a thin path runs along the steep hillside towards the quarry buildings. Passing above a small waterfall, the path then descends to the road. ⑤ Go R along grass verge and R at road junction. ⑥ At RH bend turn L (BW sign) through gate to tarmac track. ⑦ In 200yds take fence-stile (wm) on R. Bear ½ R up thin path which soon peters out. Keep on uphill to brow of hill, from where you will see, in the distance, a motor-road heading away past a farm. Aim directly for it. Cross a fence then head L, keeping nearly parallel to it, to reach stile (yellow wm) in crossfence. Descend, via two more stiles, to road and turn L. ⑧ 100yds past cattle-grid take gate/stile (wm) on R. Forward alongside wall on L (green track). Eventually wall changes to RH side of track. ⑨ At next wall-junction go R through gate/stile and diagonally L across field to walled track. Just before reaching buildings cross wall-stile (wm) on L and follow path between fence and wall. ⑩ Turn L along road to Yorkshire Water footpath sign and little step-stile. Bear R down steep field to wall-stile and descend to bottom of plantation. ⑪ Cross lane to gate/stile then double back sharp R on a lower track. Cross footbridge and follow riverside path downstream. Stay close to river, ignoring any paths forking L.

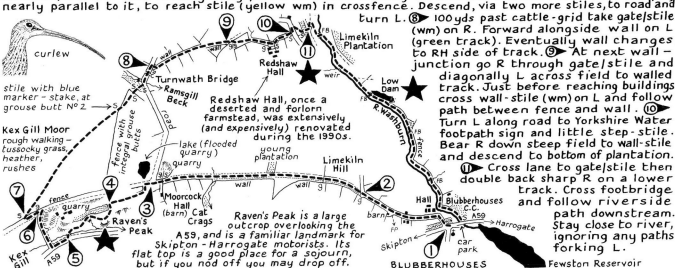

curlew

stile with blue marker - stake, at grouse butt Nº 2

Kex Gill Moor rough walking - tussocky grass, heather, rushes

Turnwath Bridge
Ramsgill Beck
road
fence with integral grouse butts

lake (flooded quarry)
quarry

Redshaw Hall

Redshaw Hall, once a deserted and forlorn farmstead, was extensively (and expensively) renovated during the 1990s.

young plantation

Limekiln Plantation
weir
Low Dam
R. Washburn
fence
FB

Limekiln Hill

wall
wall

Moorcock Hall (barn) Cat Crags

Raven's Peak

Raven's Peak is a large outcrop overlooking the A59, and is a familiar landmark for Skipton - Harrogate motorists. Its flat top is a good place for a sojourn, but if you nod off you may drop off.

Kex Gill A59

quarry

Hall
barn
FP

Blubberhouses C.C.
A59
car park
BLUBBERHOUSES
Skipton
Harrogate
Fewston Reservoir

EASY WALKING APART FROM THE JUST-UNDER-A-MILE CROSSING OF KEX GILL MOOR, WHERE HEATHER AND RUSHES CONCEAL BOG-HOLES. THIS SECTION CAN BE AVOIDED (AND *SHOULD* BE IN MIST) BY TAKING A SHORT CUT (SEE ROUTE DIRECTIONS). THIS IS DECIDEDLY A WALK OF TWO HALVES. THE SOMEWHAT BLEAK MOORLAND TERRAIN GIVES WAY AT POINT ⑧ TO VERDANT PASTURES AND A BLISSFUL FINAL MILE ALONG THE BOSKY BANKS OF THE SPARKLING WASHBURN. NO LADDER-STILES. ¾ MILE ON VERY QUIET MOTOR-ROADS, BUT THE WALK CALLS FOR TWO PERILOUS CROSSINGS OF THE A59 RACETRACK. AN ABILITY TO SPRINT TO OLYMPIC STANDARD WOULD BE ADVANTAGEOUS.

The best time to do this walk is MAY, when the moorland skies resound with the joyful song of curlew, lapwing and skylark, the hillsides are ablaze with gorse, and fragrant bluebells carpet the shady riverbanks.

FEWSTON RESERVOIR WAS COMPLETED IN 1879. IF YOU VISIT ITS SHORES, LOOK OUT FOR THE GREAT CRESTED GREBE, A HANDSOME BIRD WHICH IN SPRING IS GIVEN TO EXTRAORDINARY AND COLOURFUL DISPLAYS OF HEAD-SHAKING.

BLUBBERHOUSES

This tiny village is much prettier than its name, which tends to elicit a certain amount of jocularity. There are conflicting theories as to the origin of the name. Some would aver that 'Blubber' is a corruption of 'bilberry', whilst a more fanciful suggestion is that it refers to the weeping, or 'blubbering', of 19th C. mill children (see below). Experts, however, insist that the name means 'Black Hill Houses'. ST. ANDREW'S CHURCH was built as a chapel-of-ease to Fewston Parish Church, and was consecrated by the Bishop of Ripon on 24th September 1856. In the days when the reservoirs were being built (1870s) the 'navvies' attended the church in large numbers. BLUBBERHOUSES HALL, though of 17th C appearance, was built in 1846 on the site of an older house. It has a very fine façade of gables and stone-mullioned windows.

The stile into the Washburn plantations

LOW DAM, an old mill pond, is an ideal habitat for waterfowl. This little stone building at the foot of the lake makes an excellent birdwatchers' hide.

The pavilion, Blubberhouses C.C.

BLUBBERHOUSES C.C. play in the Nidderdale League, which is blessed with a profusion of rustic and picturesque grounds. The Blubberhouses ground occupies the site of the late and unlamented Westfield Mill. This mill – the largest in the Washburn area – operated from the end of the 1700s to the latter half of the 19th C., and relied heavily on child labour. Many of these piteous mites were homeless orphans, or waifs and strays from the work-house. They were squalidly billeted in two houses (one for boys, one for girls) on nearby Hardisty Hill, endured a 76-hour week of working drudgery, and were habitually treated with callousness and cruelty.

P Burtersett, signposted from the A684 one mile E of Hawes. Parking space at top end of village, where road bends L. Grid ref: 891 892

ROUTE DIRECTIONS

①► The walk begins at a wall-stile (FP Marsett 2) by a small barn. Forward over fence-stile (Note: This is the only fence encountered; all other field boundaries on the map are walls) and follow wall to stile at end of field. Bear slightly L up to next stile, then make for LH end of plantation (stile). ②► Bear slightly L then climb up centre of field (sketchy path). Cross broken wall and straight on over low ridge to stile. ③► Keep straight on, crossing small stream, and over another ridge to stile, beyond which is a good green path. ④► Turn R along broad, walled track (Roman road). ⑤► Keep a lookout over the wall on the L for a small sheepfold at the top of a ruined wall. A few yards beyond it a thin path rises R, passing a small upright stone and several shakeholes. Just over the skyline is the summit cairn of Drumaldrace. Bear L to return to the Roman road. ⑥► Where the track becomes enclosed turn R (BW sign) and follow wall on L (Note: At Flint Hill the official right-of-way turns R across the moor (see map) but is very boggy and difficult to follow. It's much easier to stay with the wallside path, which passes through a small quarry.) ⑦► 300 yards beyond the quarry go L through metal gate and along sunken path. A good green path winds down to a gap in wall on L. ⑧► Path passes close to hut and soon develops into a broad track which becomes increasingly stony as it descends towards Burtersett. ⑨► Enter a lane and at its end bear R.

Small barn near point ②

Map labels

A684 ①
BURTERSETT
Countersett
small barn
⑨
ruined wall
barn
broken wall
②
③
Burtersett High Pasture
stony track
Yorburgh
FP
broad track
Horton Gill
unsightly hut
⑧
Marsett
⑦
Cam High Road
④
small quarry
shakehole
R.o.W
Flint Hill
Marsett BW Crag Side Road
swallow hole
Wether Fell Side
ruins
Wether Fell
ruined wall
broken wall
Semerwater appears
wall
boggy
DRUMALDRACE 2015'
Roman Road
Silka Side
⑤
fold
⑥
Langstrothdale

NOTE
There is no official right-of-way from the Roman Road to the summit, but most passers-by will make the short detour. As long as you behave yourself there should be no objection.

A SATISFYING CIRCUIT FOR SEEKERS OF SOLITUDE AND LOVERS OF LONELY PLACES. THE FIRST MILE INVOLVES A STEADY CLIMB OF 600' UP HILLSIDE PASTURES TO THE ROMAN ROAD, WHICH IS THEN FOLLOWED FOR 1¾ MILES AS IT GENTLY RISES TO ITS HIGHEST POINT OF 1935'. THE ENTIRE ASCENT, BEING PRACTICALLY DEVOID OF INTERESTING FEATURES, OFFERS LITTLE BUT THE EXERCISE OF PUTTING ONE FOOT IN FRONT OF THE OTHER – A NOT INCONSIDERABLE PLEASURE – BUT THE DESCENT PROVIDES MAGNIFICENT VIEWS ACROSS WENSLEYDALE. SKETCHY PATH TO POINT ④; THEREAFTER GOOD CLEAR TRACKS. GENERALLY FIRM UNDERFOOT, BUT SOME SQUELCHY GROUND WILL BE ENCOUNTERED BETWEEN POINTS ⑥ AND ⑦. NO LADDER-STILES OR MOTOR-ROADS. AN EXPOSED WALK – AVOID IN BAD WEATHER.

4

MAP D

BURTERSETT

is a tranquil and attractive village set on Wensleydale's southern slopes well above the valley floor. Its cottages and farms are closely grouped along a rising lane, at the top of which is a tiny green. The village's name indicates its Norse origins. 'Sett' is a corruption of 'soetre' – a farm – and the suffix also occurs in the neighbouring settlements of Marsett and Countersett. During the 18th and 19th centuries Burtersett was a centre for the cottage industry of hand-knitting, using wool spun in the mills of West Burton and Askrigg.

THE ROMAN ROAD

Between points ④ and ⑥ we follow a section of a Roman highway which led from the fort at Bainbridge (Virosidum) to Lancaster and was constructed under the direction of Julius Agricola (Governor of Britain 78-85AD) as part of his campaign to subdue the revolting natives. In the 18th C. the route was modified to become part of the Richmond-Lancaster turnpike road. Today it provides a walkers' route from Ribblehead to Wensleydale, and is an exhilarating high-level march – although the Romans probably didn't think so.

DRUMALDRACE – THE SUMMIT OF WETHER FELL

DRUMALDRACE

DRUMALDRACE IS THE NAME OF THE SUMMIT; THE MOUNTAIN IS CALLED WETHER FELL (a wether is a castrated ram). WE HAVE CLIMBED IT ALMOST FROM VALLEY LEVEL, BUT THERE'S A MUCH EASIER WAY UP. FROM THE JUNCTION OF THE HAWES/KETTLEWELL ROAD AND THE ROMAN ROAD, TO THE SW, THE WALK TO THE SUMMIT IS LITTLE MORE THAN A MILE AND ENTAILS AN ASCENT OF BARELY 250'. THIS EASE OF ACCESS HAS RESULTED IN WETHER FELL BECOMING A FAVOURITE HAUNT OF HANG-GLIDERS.

Wheatear ♂

As you tramp these lonely hillsides, look out for the WHEATEAR, a summer visitor easily recognised by its conspicuous white rump displayed in flight. The handsome male has prominent black cheek-stripes.

5 MARBLE STEPS POT 5½ MILES

P Masongill, off the A65 2 miles NW of Ingleton. Space for two or three cars by the telephone box at the N end of the village. **PLEASE TAKE CARE NOT TO CAUSE ANY OBSTRUCTION.** Grid ref: 664 754

ROUTE DIRECTIONS

① Start along the road to the L (east) of the telephone box. Take stile on L (FP West Gate 1¼). Follow garden fence to its corner, then straight on to pass RH end of wall (wall-corner). Descend to farmyard entrance. ② Take ladder-stile on R and follow wall/fence on L uphill. At top of field turn R to ladder-stile and forward with wall on L. ③ Go straight through farmyard to ladder-stile ahead and continue forward alongside wall. Approaching next farm cross to other side of wall (gated stile) and follow it to stile in corner. ④ Go L up tarmac lane. Ignore rough track forking L. Turn L (SP Dent 8½) at T-junction. ⑤ Take ladder-stile on L by hawthorn (FP Turbary Road ⅜) and climb steeply to ladder-stile on skyline. ⑥ Bear R to climb by wall on R (when above the steep outcrops you can make a short detour L to inspect the Cheese Press Stone). ⑦ Turn L along cart-track. (For a detour to see the spectacular Rowten Pot, follow the track R from point ⑦ – 2 miles there and back). ⑧ Cross ladder-stile on R and climb rough pasture to stand of trees marking position of Marble Steps Pot. ⑨ Return alongside dry valley to visit Low Douk Cave (near wall), then rejoin the track at point ⑧ and follow it down to a water treatment works. Continue down tarmac lane to Masongill.

NOTE: MARBLE STEPS POT IS ON PRIVATE LAND, BUT THE FARMER AT MASONGILL HALL – AN AMIABLE CHAP – IS QUITE HAPPY TO ALLOW ACCESS TO SENSIBLE, WELL-BEHAVED WALKERS (e.g. users of J. Keighley's guidebooks).

MASONGILL HALL ✠

(rebuilt 1832) is a very ordinary-looking farmhouse, but has a colourful history spanning many centuries. Behind the house, on private land, the sites of a Saxon roundhouse and a medieval fortified manor house are discernible. During the Civil War the manor house belonged to the Royalist Bannister family, who paid the price for their allegiance to the Crown by having their home destroyed by Cromwell's roundheads. A barn in the farmyard has a datestone inscribed MB (Marmaduke Bannister) 1649.

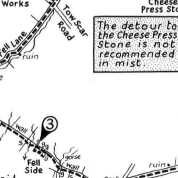

MARBLE STEPS POT
Little Pot
Large Pot
Low Douk Cave
Rowten Pot 1m
Turbary Road
Cheese Press Stone
The detour to the Cheese Press Stone is not recommended in mist.
Water Treatment Works
Tow Scar Road
Masongill Fell Lane
ruin
gorse
Parr Bank Farm
Masongill Hall
MASONGILL
A65
farm road
Fell Side
Westgate Farm
Mayfield
gorse
ruin
Radio Station
a structure of outrageous ugliness
wall
fence

20

AN INTERESTING EXPLORATION OF SOME OF KINGSDALE'S MAGNIFICENT LIMESTONE TERRAIN, CULMINATING IN A VISIT TO ONE OF YORKSHIRE'S BEST-KNOWN AND MOST IMPRESSIVE POTHOLES. A CLIMB OF 650' FROM WESTGATE FARM TO THE TURBARY ROAD INCLUDES A STEEP, ROUGH SECTION AROUND POINT ⑥. THE WALK IS SAFE IN MIST AND GENERALLY DRY UNDERFOOT, EXCEPT FOR THE BOTTOM END OF THE 'MARBLE STEPS FIELD', WHICH CAN BE A QUAGMIRE. NOT THE BEST OF WALKS FOR FIDO, THERE BEING NO FEWER THAN NINE LADDER-STILES. THERE'S AN UNAVOIDABLE TWO MILES OF TARMAC WALKING, BUT THE ROADS ARE VIRTUALLY TRAFFIC-FREE.

5

MAP A

KINGSDALE

This wild and lonely upland valley is a geological classic. From the slopes of Whernside at its head it runs almost level and straight as an arrow for three miles, its steep sides lined with limestone scars riddled with caves and potholes. The mouth of the valley is partially blocked by a small hillock of glacial debris, and it seems highly probable that Kingsdale once contained a lake. Pause awhile by the ladder-stile at point ⑥ to gaze upon the lovely scene. The hordes of walkers threading their way around the far corner of the valley will be enjoying the famous Ingleton Waterfalls Walk.

✳

THE TURBARY ROAD, NOW A SPLENDID HIGH-LEVEL WALKERS' PATH, WAS ORIGINALLY USED TO TRANSPORT PEAT DOWN FROM THE TURBARY PASTURE, WHICH IS JUST OVER TWO MILES NE OF POINT ⑦.

MARBLE STEPS POT

A small stand of trees on an otherwise bare moor indicates the position of the huge dry rift containing this classic pothole. To scramble down into this cleft looks easy, but it aint, so don't. The pot's entrance passage is an inclined and stepped tunnel; a giant staircase of highly polished black limestone which gives the pot its name. The once-powerful stream which bored this tunnel is now but a trickle, and sinks a few yards above the rift. The black steps descend for almost 200', but the whole complex system of chambers and passages drops to a depth of over 400'. In the field below Marble Steps, in a huge shakehole, is **RIFT POT**, which has an artificially enlarged entrance.

The Cheese Press Stone

These angular boulders were probably deposited here by a retreating glacier. The larger block is 9' high and weighs 15 tons.

LITTLE POT is larger than **LARGE POT**! The former is a prominent open shaft, whilst the latter has a tiny entrance covered by an iron trapdoor.

LOW DOUK CAVE

HAS AN ATTRACTIVE ENTRANCE MUCH FREQUENTED BY RABBITS. THE SOUND OF AN UNDERGROUND WATERFALL EMANATES FROM ITS SHADOWY DEPTHS. ____

ROUTE DIRECTIONS

P Kirkby Malzeard. Just W of village centre the road is wide enough to allow roadside parking. Be sure to park considerately, so as not to cause inconvenience or obstruction. *Grid ref : 234 743*

① From market cross start along Galphay/Grantley road. At cemetery gates turn R along lane. ② At L bend take gate/stile on R (FP Kirkby Malzeard) and turn L (FP sign). Follow hedge on L, crossing several intervening stiles. ③ Turn L down lane to Laverton. ④ Cross bridge and immediately go L through stile (FP sign). Follow river, then through stile to path between hedge and wire fence. Continue forward with fence on L. ⑤ From stile at fence-corner go L to gate (wm) at RH end of plantation. At end of walled path continue forward alongside hedge/fence on R. ⑥ Pass to R of farm and straight on up farm road, which soon bends R. ⑦ 150yds past bend take stile on L. Go straight across three fields, via hedge-stiles. In fourth field walk to barn then ½ L to stile. Forward with wall on R to gate (wm) into enclosed path, then R along drive. ⑧ Turn L along road, cross bridge and in 50yds go R through gate (FP sign). Climb to stile in wall. Cross lane to stile and forward with hedge on L. At end of field take RH of two gates. Forward with hedge on R, then cross next field to stile at far RH corner. ⑨ Go L along field to gate at LH corner of farm buildings and out onto road. Go L along Ripon road and L at junction (Kirkby Malzeard 2). ⑩ At Tennis Club go through big gates of Braithwaite Hall Estate and follow track. ⑪ Cross cattle-grid and turn R along farm track. Keep R at fork to double gate. Follow fence on R to enter enclosed track. ⑫ At junction turn sharp L to pass in front of cottage. Follow broad path through wood to metal gate at far end. ⑬ Cross field to stile by tree at far RH corner. Straight across three more fields to stile at RH end of wood. ⑭ Follow LH boundary through two more fields. ⑮ Bear

*This stile (marked *) utilizes an old tree stump*

Mowbray Castle (site of)
Creets Bridge
copse
Azerley
Queen's Head
KIRKBY MALZEARD
Farm road
barn
fence
⑫
⑬
The Lake
Meth Church 1880
Lawnwith Farm
metal fence
⑮ ⑭
Mill Farm
①
Hubber Wood
Holly Bank
cemetery
Hubber Lane
Deep Ghyll Farm
③ ④ ②
hedge
LAVERTON
lake
Dutch barn
⑪
Large flocks (gaggles?) of geese may be seen in the vicinity of Braithwaite Hall
R.Laver
⑤
Missies
Braithwaite Hall
farm road
fence
Laver House
The Watermill
lane
Plover Hill Farm
tennis
⑩
Inn
GALPHAY
⑥
ruin
weir
barn
pond
hedge
⑧
R.Laver
⑨
farm
⑦

VERY EASY LEVEL WALKING THROUGH PASTURES AND PARKLAND IN THE ATTRACTIVELY WOODED ROLLING COUNTRYSIDE AT THE EASTERN FRINGE OF THE DALES. BEST DONE IN AUTUMN FOR THE RICHLY GLOWING COLOURS. IN SUMMER SOME OF THE FIELDS WILL HAVE CROPS ; IN WINTER YOU COULD WALLOW IN MUD. NO LADDER-STILES, BUT MULTITUDINOUS FENCE-STILES AND GATES (44 TO BE PRECISE). 1¼ MILES ON MOTOR-ROADS. PUB HALFWAY ROUND — ALWAYS A PLUS FACTOR.

slightly R, passing tree with wm, to metal gate (wm). Follow edge of wood to swing-gate. Go R along farm road then L along road to return to Kirkby Malzeard.

KIRKBY MALZEARD

Market Cross

This ancient village, whose name is pronounced 'Malzard', was granted a market charter by Edward I in 1307. The MARKET CROSS was rebuilt in 1868, the original cross having been destroyed in the dead of night by a retired schoolmaster who considered that it ruined the view from his cottage window. (Funny folk, retired schoolmasters). This act of wanton vandalism somewhat upset the village bigwigs, who vented their spleen on the miscreant by making him demolish his cottage, which they claimed was encroaching onto the market place. ST. ANDREW'S CHURCH dates from 1150 and retains a few Norman fragments, including a lovely doorway, but the roof and interior were completely rebuilt after a disastrous fire gutted the building in 1908. Kirkby Malzeard once handled lead from the mines of Upper Nidderdale, and over the years has been involved in the manufacture of such diverse products as felt hats, clocks, woollen goods and cheese. In 1976 the famous crooner Bing Crosby, who was fond of shooting on nearby Dallowgill Moor, gave the village £1,250 for a new playing field.

MOWBRAY CASTLE was the medieval home of the de Mowbrays, Lords of the Manor. After the anarchy of Stephen's reign (1135-54), Henry II demolished 375 'illegal' castles, including this one. Only a well and a few stones remain.

Unfortunately the fine houses at Braithwaite Hall (17th C) and Azerley are not well-seen on the walk. Azerley Chase was the home of Col. R.E.B. Crompton — soldier, electrician, inventor and eccentric — who installed the first electric lights at Windsor Castle and Buckingham Palace. He formed his own company — Crompton and Co.— and his London home was the first house in England to have electric lighting. He died in 1940 aged 94.

Henry II (1154-89)

The bridge over the River Laver at Laverton. The Laver flows on to Ripon, where it joins the Skell and then the Ure.

P Dent. Large car park (pay and display) near western end of the town. Grid ref: 704 871

ROUTE DIRECTIONS

① Start along lane almost opposite car park entrance. Pass The Green and keep straight on uphill (BW Flinter Gill). **②** At T-junction of tracks turn R (BW Keldishaw 1½ ML). **③** Turn R along tarmac lane. **④** Take gate on L (FP Underwood 1½ M). Path keeps L of limestone outcrops and drops to gate/ladder-stile in far corner. **⑤** Follow wall on L through rushy area. Clear path develops and swings R along base of steep hillside. **⑥** Go round far side of ruined farmhouse to a sketchy, descending path (large farm in view ahead across the dale). Go through gap in ruined wall and descend to another gap in a more substantial one. Heading straight for house in trees, pass large oak and drop to tiny slab bridge over stream. Climb steep bank (mind the nettles), pass between buildings and straight on down farm access road. **⑦** Turn R along tarmac lane to Gawthrop. **⑧** At far end of village turn R (FP Dent ¾) up tarmac lane. At Gawthrop Hall bear R (wm) to pass to R of farm buildings then fork L to pass in front of white cottage. **⑨** Pass barn and straight on along RH edge of two fields. Straight on across two more fields to gate by ash tree. Follow cart-track down to farm. **⑩** At far end of farmyard go L through small metal gate and drop to stile at far RH corner. Forward with wall on L to gated stile. Pass round LH side of modern barn then go forward to buildings and lane curving L past Methodist Church. Turn R into Dent.

Map labels:
tiny slab bridge · Bower Bank · Tofts · gaps in walls · barn · Combe House (ruin) · Underwood · Foulsyke Farm · GAWTHROP · barn · car park, toilets, picnic area · DENT · Combe Scar · lovely green path. superb views of Dentdale · wall · rushes · limestone outcrops · Mill Beck Farm · Zion Chapel 1835 · barn · wall · Barbondale Road · kiln · sheep pens · High Laithe Gill · South Lord's Land · slab of Dent marble · Green Lane (track) · seat (for which you'll be truly thankful) · ignore walled track branching L · Flinter Gill · barn

AVOID THIS WALK IN VERY WET WEATHER (UNLESS YOU HAVE A PENCHANT FOR ANKLE-DEEP MUD)

Adam Sedgwick 1785-1873

THE MEMORIAL FOUNTAIN

stands in Dent's Main Street. Fashioned from a slab of Shap granite, it commemorates the town's most illustrious son, Adam Sedgwick. Born in Dent, where his father was both vicar and schoolmaster, Sedgwick was for many years Professor of Geology at Cambridge University, and is regarded as one of the greatest geologists of the 19th C. The fountain was Dent's principal water supply until the 1920s.

EXPLORE THE TWISTING COBBLED STREETS OF A 'TIME-WARP TOWNSHIP' AND SAMPLE THE ELYSIAN CHARMS OF THE LOWER REACHES OF DENTDALE, A SEQUESTERED VALLEY WHICH MUST SURELY RANK AS ONE OF THE LOVELIEST OF THE YORKSHIRE DALES. THE INITIAL CLIMB BY FLINTER GILL IS QUITE A HARD SLOG, BUT FROM POINT ② ONWARDS THE GOING IS VERY EASY. ONE OF THE WALK'S HIGHLIGHTS IS AN INTIMATE, CLOSE-UP VIEW OF THE BLACK, BROODING CRAGS OF THE GLACIAL COMBE SCAR. I LADDER-STILE (WITH ADJACENT GATE) AND JUST OVER HALF-A-MILE ON VERY QUIET MOTOR-ROADS.

DENT

Only a village size-wise, but historically known as 'Dent Town', this quaint place is an anachronism with an almost medieval flavour. ST. ANDREW'S CHURCH was founded in Norman times, but the present building dates largely from the 15th C. The floor of the chancel is of Dent marble, and there are some monogrammed Jacobean box pews. In the churchyard stands the OLD GRAMMAR SCHOOL, endowed by James I in 1604. The school's last pupil said goodbye in 1897. The SUN INN (first mentioned 1780) and the GEORGE AND DRAGON serve excellent ale from their own Dent Brewery. In the 18th C. Dent had a flourishing cottage industry producing knitted woollen gloves and stockings. So great was the locals' output that the phrase 'the terrible knitters e' Dent' referred to their fervour rather than their competence.

★ **GREEN LANE**, ALSO KNOWN AS OCCUPATION ROAD, HAS, OVER THE YEARS, BEEN USED TO TRANSPORT COAL AND DENT MARBLE QUARRIED AT BINKS, 1½ MILES SE OF POINT ②.

GAWTHROP

A picturesque little village whose name comes from the Norse and means 'cuckoo farm'. A corn mill was built here in the 15th C. and survived until 1876, when it was dismantled and sold to a stonemason for £50.

The road to Flinter Gill

FLINTER GILL is a beautifully wooded little gorge down which a stream tumbles prettily over a series of rock ledges. The track alongside is part of an old packhorse route to Ingleton, and is in places a treadmill of loose stones – slippery when wet and b*!!** hard work on a hot day.

BOWER BANK. This lovely old house was recorded in 1505

★ **COMBE SCAR** is a huge glacial hollow backed by a semi-circular precipice of dark Silurian rock. **COMBE HOUSE**, which dates from the 17th C., has been unoccupied for half a century. The sad ruins are a home for jackdaws and swallows. ★

ROUTE DIRECTIONS

1 Start along path by small barn (FP Muker). **2** Fork L (PW sign) down to footbridge. Climb to cross bridge above waterfall (East Gill Force) and continue along broad path. **3** Fork L up track to ruined Crackpot Hall. Continue up past another derelict farm to gate in wall. Follow narrow path up Swinner Gill. **4** At bridge turn R. 100yds above ruins ford stream to clear path slanting R up hillside. Path eventually drops slightly to ladder-stile. **5** Maintain direction. Keep to high ground, ignoring any paths heading down slope on R. **6** Cross Arn Gill, (identified by old mine level and barn). For SHORT CUT descend gill to prominent green path. This leads down to the footbridge at point **10** and reduces walk to 6½ miles. For full walk continue on high-level path. **7** When ruined wall on R turns downhill keep straight on past marker-post. Path rises slightly to run between scar and wall. Keep straight on to pass short, isolated wall. Beyond it a sketchy path descends gradually through rushes. **8** Turn sharp R along tarmac lane. Keep R at fork. **9** Ignore farm road going L. Go straight on along cart-track, then double back sharp L at a track junction and cross Rampsholme Bridge. **10** Follow path upstream to a barn. **11** Turn L round far end of barn to follow green path which soon becomes enclosed. **12** Turn R up steep farm road. When it turns L through gate marked 'PRIVATE' keep straight on up walled track. **13** At top of track bear R up green path (PW sign) to stile. Follow clear, high-level path. **14** Go R through gap in wall (PW sign). Go L at junction to follow path back to Keld.

The famous **SWALEDALE SHEEP** can be recognised by its black face with white snout. It is a tough and hardy creature well able to survive harsh winters on the highest moorland grazing. The coarse wool is ideal for carpet-making. Swaledales cross well with other breeds, and are good to keep as they tend to stick to their own small area of fell.

POSSIBLY THE MOST BEAUTIFUL – AND CERTAINLY THE MOST SPECTACULAR – WALK IN THIS BOOK. STRENUOUS, WITH ABOUT 1000' OF ASCENT WHICH INCLUDES A FAIRLY GRUELLING 500' SLOG FROM POINT ⑫ UP THE SIDE OF KISDON. THE PATHS, THOUGH GENERALLY VERY CLEAR, DEMAND GOOD BOOTS AND THE UTMOST CARE, BEING IN PLACES NARROW AND SLIPPERY, WITH HAIR-RAISING DECLIVITIES ON THE R.(ACROPHOBIA AND VERTIGO SUFFERERS MAY FEEL UNCOMFORTABLE). NO MOTOR-ROADS, AND ONLY TWO LADDER-STILES. EXQUISITE BIRD'S-EYE VIEWS AND VAST PANORAMAS ACROSS THE MOORS.

8

MAP D

★ **SWALEDALE** has a wild, rugged, almost austere beauty quite unmatched by any other dale, and the section just below Keld, where the Swale plunges and tumbles through a wooded limestone gorge, is the valley's *pièce de résistance*. This walker's paradise is, in the author's humble opinion, the loveliest square mile in the Yorkshire Dales.

SWINNER GILL
This awesome, crag-lined ravine was once a flourishing lead-mining centre. The industry died out in the late 19thC., leaving a scene of widespread devastation, and scars that nature has not yet managed to heal. The ruined SMELT MILL, which worked from 1769 to c1820, had two rooms. The RH room (as seen facing the ruin with your back to the stream) contained the smelting hearths, whilst in the LH room were the bellows, driven by a waterwheel. Visible behind the mill are the remains of a long 'flue' which carried toxic fumes up onto the moor. SWINNER GILL KIRK is a cave beside a waterfall at the head of a limestone gorge. It is said (though it sounds a bit far-fetched) that secret services were held in the cave by nonconformists in the 1660s, when their religion was illegal.

The rusting remains of a tractor near Crackpot Hall.

KELD This tiny, haphazard cluster of grey buildings – Swaledale's uppermost settlement – has its roots in Viking times, and in the Middle Ages was called Appletreekeld ('Keld' is Old Norse for 'spring' or 'well'.) 'Day-walkers' flock here in droves, and footsore Pennine Way and Coast-to-Coast pilgrims recharge their batteries at the popular Youth Hostel. The lure of Keld is the rushing river with its series of attractive falls and cataracts. Wain Wath Force, Catrake Force, Kisdon Force and East Gill Force are all close by, although the latter, on a small tributary stream, is the only one seen on this particular walk.

East Gill Force

Looking up to Kisdon Cottage (*a house with a wonderful view*)

KISDON is an isolated, steep-sided hill rising to a height of 1636'. The Pennine Way follows a natural limestone shelf along its eastern flank – a superb, airy terrace high above the Swale. This is one of the finest sections of the Pennine Way's 270-300+ miles (*length of route depends on how many times you get lost*).

CRACKPOT HALL was abandoned in 1953 because of mining subsidence. The name did not refer to the mental state of its occupants; 'Crackpot' means 'pothole of the crows.'

AROUND MUKER ARE SOME OF THE FINEST TRADITIONAL HAY MEADOWS IN THE DALES

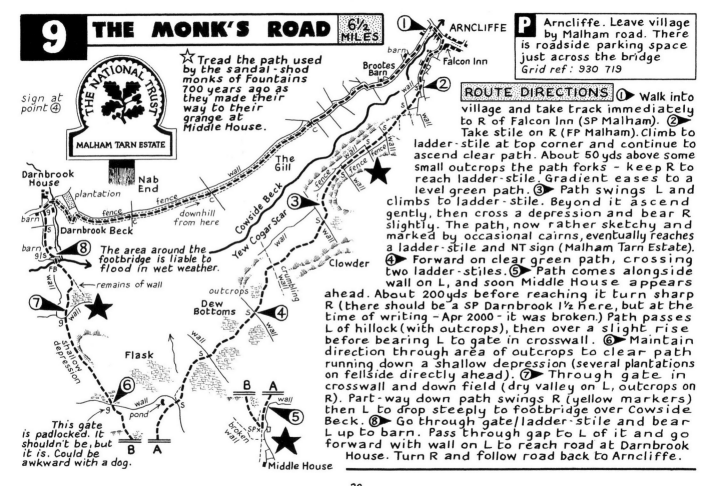

9 THE MONK'S ROAD 6½ MILES

☆ Tread the path used by the sandal-shod monks of Fountains 700 years ago as they made their way to their grange at Middle House.

THE NATIONAL TRUST
MALHAM TARN ESTATE

sign at point ④

ARNCLIFFE
barn
Brootes Barn
Falcon Inn

Darnbrook House
plantation
Nab End
The Gill
Cowside Beck
fence
downhill from here
barn
Darnbrook Beck
barn

⑧ The area around the footbridge is liable to flood in wet weather.

FB
remains of wall

⑦
shallow depression

Flask

⑥
wall
pond

This gate is padlocked. It shouldn't be, but it is. Could be awkward with a dog.

B A

Yew Cogar Scar
③
Clowder
crumbling wall
outcrops
Dew Bottoms
④

B A
broken wall
SP
⑤
Middle House

ROUTE DIRECTIONS

① Walk into village and take track immediately to R of Falcon Inn (SP Malham). ② Take stile on R (FP Malham). Climb to ladder-stile at top corner and continue to ascend clear path. About 50 yds above some small outcrops the path forks – keep R to reach ladder-stile. Gradient eases to a level green path. ③ Path swings L and climbs to ladder-stile. Beyond it ascend gently, then cross a depression and bear R slightly. The path, now rather sketchy and marked by occasional cairns, eventually reaches a ladder-stile and NT sign (Malham Tarn Estate). ④ Forward on clear green path, crossing two ladder-stiles. ⑤ Path comes alongside wall on L, and soon Middle House appears ahead. About 200 yds before reaching it turn sharp R (there should be a SP Darnbrook 1½ here, but at the time of writing – Apr 2000 – it was broken.) Path passes L of hillock (with outcrops), then over a slight rise before bearing L to gate in crosswall. ⑥ Maintain direction through area of outcrops to clear path running down a shallow depression (several plantations on fellside directly ahead). ⑦ Through gate in crosswall and down field (dry valley on L, outcrops on R). Part-way down path swings R (yellow markers) then L to drop steeply to footbridge over Cowside Beck. ⑧ Go through gate/ladder-stile and bear L up to barn. Pass through gap to L of it and go forward with wall on L to reach road at Darnbrook House. Turn R and follow road back to Arncliffe.

A FABULOUS WALK, WITH A WHOLE SUCCESSION OF SPLENDID VIEWPOINTS, THROUGH THE STUNNING LIMESTONE SCENERY OF GLORIOUS LITTONDALE. GENERALLY EASY WALKING, BUT THERE IS A SHORT, STEEP CLIMB UP THE HILLSIDE FROM POINT ② AND ANOTHER UP THE TARMAC ROAD FROM DARNBROOK. 10 LADDER-STILES (WHICH COULD PRESENT A PROBLEM IF YOU HAVE A HEAVY, NON-AGILE DOG). 2¼ MILES ON A QUIET MOTOR-ROAD. THE ROUTE, THOUGH FAIRLY OBVIOUS IN CLEAR WEATHER, IS NOT EASY TO FOLLOW IN THICK MIST. IN SUCH CONDITIONS IT WOULD BE WISE TO BE EQUIPPED WITH A COMPASS – OR WISER STILL TO COME BACK ON A DAY WHEN YOU CAN SEE WHERE YOU'RE GOING.

LITTONDALE

LITTONDALE is a U-shaped glacial valley drained by the Skirfare, a river with a habit of disappearing underground. In Norman times it was a hunting forest, before becoming a huge sheep-rearing estate of the wealthy Fountains Abbey. Littondale is noted for its superb field barns, and is one of the few dales unscarred by the ravages of lead-mining.

collapsed signpost near Middle House

ARNCLIFFE

ARNCLIFFE, the major settlement of Littondale, was founded way back in Saxon times and features in the Domesday Book. It is an attractive little village of grey cottages grouped around a spacious green which sports a stone water-pump of mid-19th C. vintage. Arncliffe was the first setting for the soap opera 'Emmerdale Farm' (now 'Emmerdale'), and the Falcon Inn was the original 'Woolpack'.

ST. OSWALD'S CHURCH occupies a site on which a stone church has stood since c1100. About 1500 this church was partially demolished and rebuilt ; of this church only the tower remains. Further rebuilding took place in 1796 and 1841. Inside the church is a list of Littondale men who fought in 1513 in the Battle of Flodden Field on the Scottish border.

☆

THE ROAD WALK

THE ROAD WALK No right-of-way exists along Cowside Beck, which is a shame, as it would have provided a highly spectacular finish and made this walk one of the very finest in the Dales. The only option – a return from Darnbrook by road – is, however, by no means unpleasant, apart from the initial steep pull which will have you cursing J. Keighley. Much of the road is unenclosed, so if your feet are aching you can tread the grass verges whilst admiring the breathtaking view of Yew Cogar Scars – one of the most-photographed scenes in the Dales. Note the impressive-looking Cowside Beck Cave, high up in a rocky cove, and see if you can pick out the route of your outward journey along the limestone ledges.

DARNBROOK

DARNBROOK was a grange of Fountains Abbey. The present house dates from the 1660s. Beside the farmhouse wall is a pothole – Robinson's Pot – which leads to an extensive cave system.

Darnbrook House

10 LEAD MINES OF NIDDERDALE — 6½ MILES

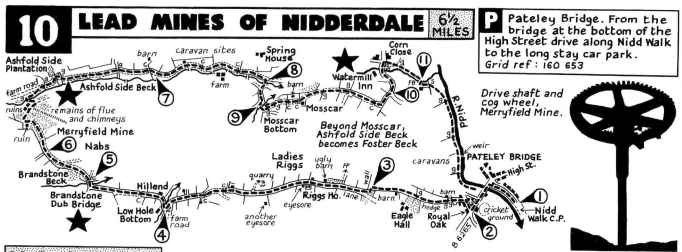

P Pateley Bridge. From the bridge at the bottom of the High Street drive along Nidd Walk to the long stay car park. Grid ref: 160 653

Drive shaft and cog wheel, Merryfield Mine.

Map labels: Ashfold Side Plantation · farm road · ruins · remains of flue and chimneys · ruin · Merryfield Mine · Nabs · Brandstone Beck · Brandstone Dub Bridge · Low Hole Bottom · farm road · Hillend · Ashfold Side Beck · barn · caravan sites · farm · Spring House · barn · Mosscar · Mosscar Bottom · Beyond Mosscar, Ashfold Side Beck becomes Foster Beck · Ladies Riggs · quarry · ugly barn · eyesore · Riggs Ho. · lane · another eyesore · Eagle Hall · Royal Oak · hedge · barn · Watermill Inn · Corn Close · FB · R. Nidd · weir · caravans · PATELEY BRIDGE · High St. · cricket ground · B 6265 · Nidd Walk C.P.

ROUTE DIRECTIONS

① Return to bridge, cross it and straight on along main road. ② Turn R just before Royal Oak. At Chapel Mews turn L up rough lane which soon becomes a green path. Pass barn and continue uphill alongside LH field boundary. ③ Climb wall-stile on L into trees, then turn R to join tarmac lane. ④ Tarmac ends at Low Hole Bottom. Follow 'Nidderdale Way' signs. ⑤ Cross bridge and cattle-grid, then turn L (blue wm) up stony track. ⑥ Keep R (straight on) at fork. Go through a gateway to reach a large area of mine spoil. At its far side descend by some ruins to cross the beck on a concrete slab. Through gate (wm) and turn R up path. Continue R along farm track. ⑦ The track gains a tarmac surface. Keep straight on, staying on the LH side of the beck. ⑧ Go R through metal gate (yellow wm) into Low Wood Caravan Site. Cross stream, bear R up cart-track then fork L (blue arrow). ⑨ Cross footbridge and take gate immediately to R of house. Follow access drive. ⑩ Turn L along road. Pass Watermill Inn on your L, and just before reaching some farm buildings turn R (FP Pateley Bridge). Cross field to handgate and streamside path. ⑪ Cross footbridge and continue on streamside path to stile. Go ½ R across field then follow riverside path back to Pateley Bridge.

THE AWARD-WINNING **NIDDERDALE MUSEUM**, AT PATELEY BRIDGE, HAS EXHIBITS FEATURING ALL ASPECTS OF DALES LIFE, INCLUDING LEAD-MINING. OPEN EASTER TO THE END OF OCTOBER, DAILY, 2–5.

A JOYFUL CIRCUIT OF ONE OF NIDDERDALE'S LOVELIEST SIDE-VALLEYS. EXPLORE THE DECAYING REMNANTS OF A LONG-ABANDONED INDUSTRY, THEN ENJOY A NOGGIN IN THE SHADOW OF A MAGNIFICENT WATERWHEEL BEFORE COMPLETING THE WALK ALONG THE BANKS OF THE SPARKLING NIDD. EASY WALKING — MOSTLY ON TARMAC LANES OR STONY FARM TRACKS — WITH NO STEEP GRADIENTS. NO LADDER-STILES AND ONLY ⅓ MILE ON MOTOR-ROADS.

IMPORTANT NOTE: THIS WALK SHOULD BE DONE IN **DRY WEATHER**. AFTER HEAVY OR PROLONGED RAIN THE FIELDS BETWEEN POINTS ② AND ③ WILL BE VERY MUDDY, AND IT MAY BE DIFFICULT, OR IMPOSSIBLE, TO FORD ASHFOLD SIDE BECK AT THE MINES.

MAP E

War Memorial

Hillend

PATELEY BRIDGE

PATELEY BRIDGE was first recorded — as 'Patelia' — in the 12th C. In those days the settlement was probably up on the hillside near the now-ruinous St. Mary's Church (built in 1321 and replaced by St.Cuthbert's 1827). Edward II granted a Market Charter in 1320, and in the same year there was the first mention of a bridge. This would probably have been a wooden structure; the present stone bridge is 18th C., and has been widened. In the 19th C. Scotgate Ash Quarry, to the N of the town, produced large slabs of gritstone for railway platforms, dock quays and the steps of public buildings. The quarry closed down during the first World War. Pateley Bridge — the capital of Upper Nidderdale — has a good range of shops, restaurants and pubs, and is a very popular holiday centre. The author, who tends to judge a place by the quality of its fish and chips, regards Pateley Bridge as one of his favourite towns.

LEAD MINES

Lead has been obtained from this area since Roman times. Merryfield was once a prosperous and highly productive mine, its workings extending for several miles south and west beneath Greenhow Moor. Desolate spoil heaps and a few sad ruins are all that now remain. The line of the flue, with its chimneys, is quite prominent. Over a mile in length, its purpose was to carry toxic wastes and fumes from the smelt mill up onto the open moor. Across the gill is a 'hush', created by first damming a stream then allowing it to gouge out the soil in a rushing flood, thus exposing the underlying ore deposits. Explore the workings with the utmost care, and stay well away from any open shafts or levels, which are all in a dangerous condition after a century of disuse.

THE WATERMILL INN was a working flax mill until as recently as 1966. The splendidly restored wheel, which is of 1904 vintage, boasts a diameter of 35', making it one of the largest 'overshot' waterwheels in the country.

★ **HIGHLY RECOMMENDED**: A VISIT TO THE **MUSEUM OF YORKSHIRE DALES LEAD MINING** AT EARBY *(between Colne and Skipton)* OPEN APRIL – OCTOBER WED – SUN 1PM – 5PM

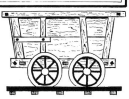

11 MAIDEN CASTLE 4¾ MILES

P Reeth. On the green at the village centre (honesty box). Grid ref: 038 994. Reeth also has a long-stay car park.

ROUTE DIRECTIONS

① Leave Reeth by the Richmond road (downhill). ② About 150 yds beyond bridge take gate on R (SP Grinton) to riverside path. Pass farm then bear L past an ash tree and round end of wall. Head for steps at end of bridge. ③ Turn R and follow road through Grinton, keeping straight on at both road-junctions. ④ In ¼ mile cross stone bridge on R and go L up cart-track to gate onto open moor. Green path bears L up hillside to crossfence with two stiles. Take LH one and keep straight on uphill. ⑤ When almost abreast of Grinton Lodge (prominent building in trees away to L) fork R onto faint path which slants up the moor towards fence on skyline. Through gate near junction of fence and wall, and forward with wall on R. When wall turns downhill keep straight on along level path through heather. ⑥ Path drops slightly to a wall-corner. Cross cart-track and straight on across rough moorland. No continuous path – maintain a level course. Eventually you'll see the huge ditch of Maiden Castle. Walk round it clockwise to a solitary hawthorn, from where clear path descends L to road. ⑦ Go L along road. ⑧ Turn sharp R (SP Grinton 2¼) to gate (wm). Path runs alongside wall on R, then drops to riverbank. ⑨ When wall on R ends, continue along riverside embankment for a short way. You now have 2 options : A. To follow official right-of-way go diagonally R across big field to gate at far corner. Go forward between wall and fence. When fence ends head L for suspension bridge. B. Simply follow riverbank. Not a right-of-way, but well-used and stiles provided. ⑩ Cross suspension bridge and turn R to gate. Follow well-trodden path along centre of field. ⑪ Go up a walled path by some barns. After turning R it becomes a tarmac lane. Keep straight on until you reach Heatherdale Bungalow (on R). Turn L here to walk along a back lane which emerges onto the green.

> **!** The right-of-way path, as it approaches point ⑨, appears to be in danger of collapsing into the river.

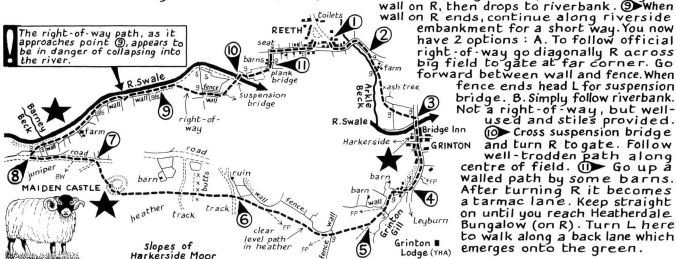

32

ROUTE - FINDING BETWEEN POINTS ⑤ AND ⑦ NEEDS SOME CARE, AND THE ½ MILE SECTION FROM POINT ⑥ TO MAIDEN CASTLE, THOUGH LEVEL, IS PATHLESS. PROGRESS HERE MAY BE LABORIOUS THROUGH DEEP HEATHER. OTHERWISE, THE WALKING IS VERY EASY, WITH NO STEEP GRADIENTS. NO LADDER-STILES. ¾ MILE ON MOTOR-ROADS. THE RIVER SCENERY IS SUPREMELY LOVELY, AND FROM THE SLOPES OF HARKERSIDE MOOR THERE ARE TREMENDOUS VIEWS OF REETH, WITH ARKENGARTHDALE BEYOND AND, TO ITS R, THE DRAMATIC, SWEEPING SKYLINE OF FREMINGTON EDGE. SOME OF THE RIVERSIDE MEADOWS ARE LIABLE TO FLOODING AFTER VERY HEAVY RAIN.

One of Reeth's many tea shops

REETH

rejoices in a beautiful setting at the confluence of Arkengarthdale and Swaledale, and is a perfect base from which to explore each of these lovely valleys. A market charter was granted in 1695, and in the 18th. and 19th. centuries Reeth was an important lead-mining centre. Since the cessation of mining activities Reeth's population has dwindled to about a quarter of its former size, but nevertheless it is regarded as the 'capital' of Upper Swaledale, and the many inns, cafés and shops around the huge, sloping green still retain an air of prosperity. At the lower end of the green is a small National Park Centre, and the Swaledale Folk Museum displays a good range of exhibits illustrating the fascinating local history of the area.

Leper's Squint

★ MAIDEN CASTLE

Don't expect to find the picturesque ruins of a Norman stronghold, or you'll be sorely disappointed. The eye of the non-expert (such as the author) will perceive only the remains of a huge circular ditch. Its origins lie obscured in the mists of time, but the general opinion is that it was built by the Brigantes c 70AD as a defence against the Roman invaders. It may, however, be much older, for excavations locally suggest that this part of Swaledale was a major settlement in the Bronze and Iron Ages.

A 'Creep Hole' or 'Cripple' in a wall allows sheep to pass between fields. This example can be seen just beyond point ⑧

GRINTON CHURCH (see frontispiece)

is an absolute gem. Dedicated to St. Andrew, and known as the 'Cathedral of the Dales', it was built by monks from Bridlington in the early 12th C. There is an original Norman window above the tower arch, but the present building is largely 15th C. The church has a Norman font, a lovely Jacobean pulpit, and a bookstand so old that it may well have been used by the monks. In the S. wall is a 'leper's squint', or 'hagioscope', through which people with contagious diseases could watch the service.

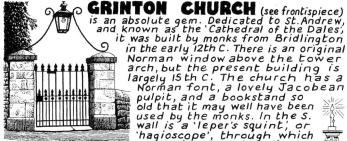

The churchyard was once the only consecrated burial ground in Swaledale, and corpses had to be carried to it for distances of up to 12 miles.

12 LOWER BISHOPDALE 6½ MILES

P Thoralby, near Aysgarth. Visitors' car park (honesty box) behind Village Hall opposite George Inn. Grid ref : 000 867

ROUTE DIRECTIONS

① From car park entrance go R then R again to walk downhill out of village. **②** Just before reaching The Old Corn Mill (flats) turn R by fence to gate (FP Littleburn ¼) and woodland path. After a stile keep straight on along LH field boundary then, in big field, bear R to follow FP signs to stile. **③** Turn L along tarmac lane, over bridge and straight on along farm track. **④** Through gate between two barns and straight on, with wall, then fence on your L. **⑤** Through facing gate and forward, with wall now on your R, to a barn. Follow farm road past a tall barn. **⑥** Turn R over cattle-grid and follow farm road to farm. **⑦** Turn R (FP sign) at first barn, then turn L alongside rear of buildings to wooden gate in crosswall. Bear slightly R, aiming for barn. **⑧** Through gate to L of it then straight on towards another barn. Maintain direction to pass through a series of wall-stiles. **⑨** Ignore gate with ornamental gateposts. Cross farm track to fence-gate, then straight ahead to pass, via gates, in front of farmhouse. Turn L down access track. **⑩** Go L along main road. In 150yds turn R over farm bridge and immediately L through gate. Follow beck to stile at bridge. **⑪** Forward along main road for 1½ miles. **⑫** Look out for slit-stile on R (easily missed). Follow direction of fingerpost (FP Newbiggin ½) diagonally up field towards small gap in line of trees. Cross small stream and forward along LH side of line of trees to slit-stile. Continue forward alongside fence on L to another cont. →

The elegant Georgian façade of Littleburn Hall

ROUTE DIRECTIONS (cont.) slit-stile, then follow wall on R to enter walled green track to Newbiggin. **⑬** Walk L along road through village. **⑭** Turn L at junction by ivy-covered Newbiggin House. Cross main road and down lane (Thoralby ½).

here the author sat on a wasps' nest — fortunately without serious consequences

to Buckden

34

👣 LOWLAND PASTURES, ROADS AND LANES. ABSURDLY EASY – ABOUT THE NEAREST YOU'LL GET TO A LEVEL WALK IN THE YORKSHIRE DALES. BISHOPDALE IS A LOVELY VALLEY AND, BEING THE EASIEST OF THE THREE ROAD ROUTES LINKING WHARFEDALE AND WENSLEYDALE, IS VERY FAMILIAR TO MOTORISTS. IT IS, HOWEVER, RELATIVELY LITTLE-FREQUENTED BY WALKERS, WHO FIND THAT A DEARTH OF RIGHTS-OF-WAY, PARTICULARLY ON THE E SIDE OF THE DALE, LIMITS THE SCOPE FOR DEVISING CIRCULAR RAMBLES. THE HIGHLIGHTS OF THIS WALK ARE TWO MELLOW VILLAGES AND A SUPERB 17TH C YEOMAN FARMHOUSE. NO LADDER-STILES, BUT SOME OF THE SLIT-STILES ARE A BIT AWKWARD FOR THOSE WHO, LIKE THE AUTHOR, ARE NOT BLESSED WITH A SYLPH-LIKE FIGURE. 2½ MILES ON MOTOR-ROADS – UNAVOIDABLE DUE TO R-O-W PROBLEMS.

BISHOPDALE

had, in Ice Age times, a glacial lake 5 miles long by 2 miles wide, the deposited silt from which has left the valley with a richly fertile soil. During the Middle Ages this was a hunting chase for deer. Bishopdale has some of the finest 17th C. farmhouses in the Yorkshire Dales.

The splendid New House Farm, dated 1635

This tablet on Littleburn Bridge commemorates the Duke of Wellington

SOLA IN DEO SALUS

Pons Egerianus incolarum viciniorum
sumptu flummi prave parvo parumper
periculosifsimo super adstructus paci saluti
sub Deo Wellingtonio sacer
Accipe dux belli quem pax petit arbiter audax
Pontigeros fluctus exilientis aquoe
Fontigenas fluctus capiet mare divitis und

THORALBY

is Bishopdale's principal village, and features in the Domesday Book. In the days when iron and lead were mined at High Scar, some three miles up-valley (above New House Farm) there were three pubs in Thoralby. The cosy George Inn (built 1732) is the only survivor.

CROOKSBY BARN

The barn marks the site of one of the Dales' lost villages. 'Crocsbi' was recorded in the Domesday Survey of 1086, but disappeared (reason unknown) in the late 13th C.

PINFOLDS

are small enclosures where stray or trespassing animals were kept until redeemed by their owners. Both Thoralby and Newbiggin have pinfolds. Thoralby's is just below the Methodist Chapel, and carries an information plaque.

NEWBIGGIN

This linear village has charming 17th and 18th C. cottages ranged along its main street. There is no through motor-road, and the place is a rather sleepy backwater, but in the 19th C. it was a busy community three times its present size, with many of its menfolk employed in the lead mines on nearby Wasset Fell. Newbiggin Feast was a grand, three-day annual event which attracted dalesfolk from miles around. It was suspended for the duration of World War I and never revived.

Brook House Farm, Newbiggin

13 THE XII APOSTLES — 5 MILES

P Ilkley. From town centre drive up Wells Road and immediately after crossing a cattle-grid turn R into a sizeable car park. *Grid ref: 117 471*

ROUTE DIRECTIONS

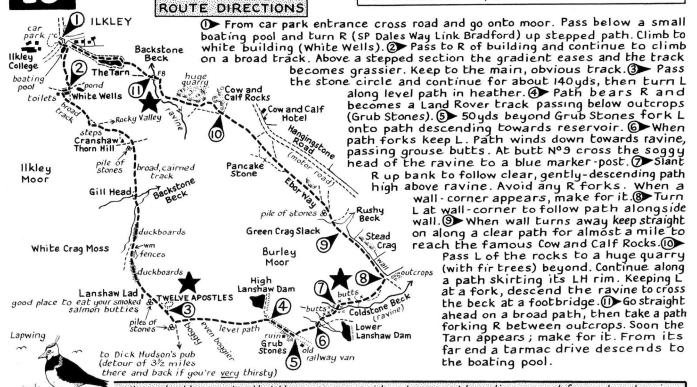

0► From car park entrance cross road and go onto moor. Pass below a small boating pool and turn R (SP Dales Way Link Bradford) up stepped path. Climb to white building (White Wells). **2►** Pass to R of building and continue to climb on a broad track. Above a stepped section the gradient eases and the track becomes grassier. Keep to the main, obvious track. **3►** Pass the stone circle and continue for about 140yds, then turn L along level path in heather. **4►** Path bears R and becomes a Land Rover track passing below outcrops (Grub Stones). **5►** 50yds beyond Grub Stones fork L onto path descending towards reservoir. **6►** When path forks keep L. Path winds down towards ravine, passing grouse butts. At butt No 9 cross the soggy head of the ravine to a blue marker-post. **7►** Slant R up bank to follow clear, gently-descending path high above ravine. Avoid any R forks. When a wall-corner appears, make for it. **8►** Turn L at wall-corner to follow path alongside wall. **9►** When wall turns away keep straight on along a clear path for almost a mile to reach the famous Cow and Calf Rocks. **10►** Pass L of the rocks to a huge quarry (with fir trees) beyond. Continue along a path skirting its LH rim. Keeping L at a fork, descend the ravine to cross the beck at a footbridge. **11►** Go straight ahead on a broad path, then take a path forking R between outcrops. Soon the Tarn appears; make for it. From its far end a tarmac drive descends to the boating pool.

Map labels: car park; ILKLEY; Ilkley College; boating pool; toilets; The Tarn; pond; White Wells; broad track; Rocky Valley; steps; Cranshaw Thorn Hill; pile of stones; broad, cairned track; Gill Head; Backstone Beck; Ilkley Moor; duckboards; wm fences; White Crag Moss; duckboards; Lanshaw Lad; *good place to eat your smoked salmon butties*; TWELVE APOSTLES; piles of stones; boggy; even boggier; level path; Lapwing; *to Dick Hudson's pub (detour of 3½ miles there and back if you're very thirsty)*; Backstone Beck; FB; huge quarry; Cow and Calf Rocks; Cow and Calf Hotel; Hangingstone Road (motor road); Pancake Stone; Ebor Way; pile of stones; Green Crag Slack; Burley Moor; Rushy Beck; Stead Crag; wall; outcrops; butts; High Lanshaw Dam; butts; Coldstone Beck (ravine); ruin; Grub Stones; old railway van; Lower Lanshaw Dam

Walkers should remember that these moors provide a home and breeding-ground for curlew, lapwing, red grouse, golden plover, skylark and many other bird-species. Please keep dogs under close control during the nesting season (April-June). Disturbance may cause nests and chicks to be abandoned.

■ ■

A SHORT BUT HIGHLY ENJOYABLE WALK ON THE MOST FAMOUS BIT OF MOORLAND IN BRITAIN. IN ADDITION TO ITS TWO MAJOR HIGHLIGHTS – A BEAUTIFULLY RESTORED GEORGIAN BATH HOUSE AND A MYSTERIOUS PREHISTORIC RELIC — THE WALK OFFERS SUPERB PANORAMIC VIEWS AND SOME HIGH QUALITY ROCK AND RAVINE SCENERY. A LONG CLIMB OF ABOUT 600' FROM THE CAR PARK TO CRANSHAW THORN HILL GETS ALL THE HARD WORK DONE WITH. NO LADDER-STILES OR MOTOR-ROADS. GOOD PATHS THROUGHOUT, BUT EXPOSED TO THE ELEMENTS AND UNPLEASANT IN MIST.

13

MAP F

♫ YORKSHIRE'S NATIONAL ANTHEM ♫

The famous song 'On Ilkla Moor Baht 'At' is said to have been written in 1886, when members of a Halifax church choir were enjoying a picnic on Ilkley Moor. During the picnic a courting couple wandered away from the group. The girl's name was Mary Jane. On their return, their fellow choristers extemporized a song to the hymn tune 'Cranbrook', beginning 'Wheear 'as ta been sin' Ah saw thee?' The second verse answers 'Tha's been a cooartin' Mary Jane'.

WHITE WELLS

was built in the 1760s as a bath house for Ilkley folk, who could there enjoy a dip in the cold but pure and supposedly curative waters of the moorland spring. The growing popularity of hydropathy in the early 19th C. turned Ilkley into a fashionable spa town, and many of its hotels and large houses date from this period. Patients were transported up the moor by donkey. The sturdy building, which still contains the original well, is now a cafe and visitor centre.

Lanshaw Lad

An old boundary stone, elaborately carved. The much eroded date may be 1833, 1837 or 1887.

THE 50' DIAMETER STONE CIRCLE KNOWN AS **THE TWELVE APOSTLES** IS OBVIOUSLY OF GREAT ANTIQUITY – BUT HOW OLD? IT MAY DATE BACK TO THE BRONZE AGE, OR POSSIBLY EVEN TO THE NEW STONE AGE (2,000 BC). AND WHAT WAS ITS PURPOSE? WAS IT A BURIAL GROUND, OR WERE THESE STONES PERHAPS PART OF SOME ANCIENT RELIGIOUS RITUAL?

MINDBENDER: How many of the 12 (Biblical) Apostles can you name? Answers below – no cheating.

Pancake Stone

from above

COW AND CALF: Famous Yorkshire landmark. Calf is huge boulder below crags – 26' high and weighs 1000 tons. **THE TARN**: Former millpond enlarged and landscaped in 1870s.

Answers : Simon (Peter), Andrew, James, John, Philip, Bartholomew, Thomas, Matthew, James (the Less), Lebbaeus, Simon (the Zealot), Judas. How did you score? Less than 5 – shameful. 5-7 Average. 8-10 Good. 11 Excellent. All 12 – you cheated.

37

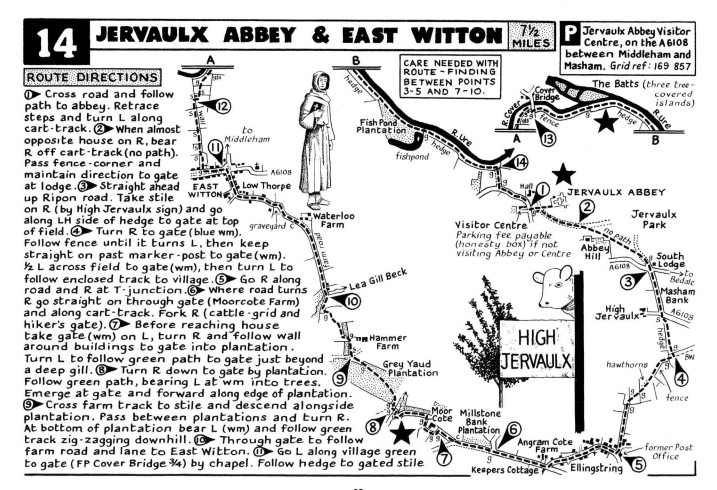

P Jervaulx Abbey Visitor Centre, on the A6108 between Middleham and Masham. Grid ref: 169 857

ROUTE DIRECTIONS

CARE NEEDED WITH ROUTE-FINDING BETWEEN POINTS 3-5 AND 7-10.

① Cross road and follow path to abbey. Retrace steps and turn L along cart-track. ② When almost opposite house on R, bear R off cart-track (no path). Pass fence-corner and maintain direction to gate at lodge. ③ Straight ahead up Ripon road. Take stile on R (by High Jervaulx sign) and go along LH side of hedge to gate at top of field. ④ Turn R to gate (blue wm). Follow fence until it turns L, then keep straight on past marker-post to gate (wm). ½ L across field to gate (wm), then turn L to follow enclosed track to village. ⑤ Go R along road and R at T-junction. ⑥ Where road turns R go straight on through gate (Moorcote Farm) and along cart-track. Fork R (cattle-grid and hiker's gate). ⑦ Before reaching house take gate (wm) on L, turn R and follow wall around buildings to gate into plantation. Turn L to follow green path to gate just beyond a deep gill. ⑧ Turn R down to gate by plantation. Follow green path, bearing L at wm into trees. Emerge at gate and forward along edge of plantation. ⑨ Cross farm track to stile and descend alongside plantation. Pass between plantations and turn R. At bottom of plantation bear L (wm) and follow green track zig-zagging downhill. ⑩ Through gate to follow farm road and lane to East Witton. ⑪ Go L along village green to gate (FP Cover Bridge ¾) by chapel. Follow hedge to gated stile

The Batts (three tree-covered islands)

to Middleham

EAST WITTON — Low Thorpe — A6108

Waterloo Farm — graveyard

Fish Pond Plantation — R. Ure — fishpond — hedge

Cover Bridge — R. Cover — fence

JERVAULX ABBEY

Visitor Centre. Parking fee payable (honesty box) if not visiting Abbey or Centre

Jervaulx Park — no path — Abbey Hill — South Lodge — to Bedale

Lea Gill Beck

farm road

Hammer Farm

Grey Yaud Plantation

HIGH JERVAULX

Masham Bank — High Jervaulx — A6108 — hedge — hawthorns — fence — BW

Moor Cote — Millstone Bank Plantation — Angram Cote Farm — former Post Office

Keepers Cottage — Ellingstring

AN EXPLORATION OF THE ATMOSPHERIC RUINS OF A GREAT CISTERCIAN ABBEY FOLLOWED BY A GENTLY UNDULATING RAMBLE THROUGH PARKLAND, PASTURES AND PLANTATIONS. AFTER VISITING ONE OF THE DISTRICT'S NEATEST AND MOST ATTRACTIVE VILLAGES, THE WALK ENDS WITH A DELIGHTFUL 1¾ MILE RIVERSIDE STROLL ALONG THE BANKS OF THE COVER AND THE URE. NO LADDER-STILES. ¾ MILE ON MOTOR-ROADS. SET ON THE EASTERNMOST FRINGE OF THE DALES, THE WALK PROVIDES SWEEPING VIEWS ACROSS THE VAST VALE OF YORK TO THE NORTH YORK MOORS.

14

MAP G

(wm), then straight on along RH edge of fields. ⑫▶ Follow FP signs round small ruined barn, down through gate in wire fence and head for bridge. Stile and gate give access to road. ⑬▶ Cross road to gate and follow obvious riverside path. ⑭▶ Turn R through gate and up cart-track to road. Turn L.

Jervaulx Abbey

lies in a beautiful parkland setting, and was founded c 1156 by Cistercian monks who had forsaken a bleak establishment near Askrigg. The abbey takes its name from a medieval French translation of valley – 'vaulx' – and the River Ure or Yore – 'Jer'. Jervaulx grew prosperous from sheep-rearing, and was renowned throughout the country for the breeding of fine horses. The monks also made cheese from ewes' milk - the original Wensleydale cheese. Disaster struck in 1536, when the abbey's treasures were seized by Henry VIII and the buildings were severely mutilated at the hands of the Crown. The last abbot, Adam Sedbergh, was executed for his part in the Pilgrimage of Grace – a protest against the Dissolution of the monasteries. **VISITOR CENTRE** Open daily Mar-Oct 10-5; Nov-Dec 12-4 (closed Mondays).

Cover Bridge

At the northern end of this graceful bridge stands the ancient and rather quaint COVERBRIDGE INN, a boozer much patronised by the angling fraternity. The 'GENTS' is dated 1674.

EAST WITTON

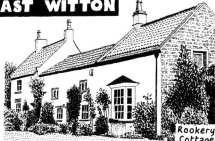

Rookery Cottage

This very attractive estate village, with its neat cottages ranged along each side of a long, sloping green, was in Norman times the largest village in Wensleydale. East Witton gained a Market Charter in 1307, but its market ceased to function in the 18th C. The dreaded bubonic plague swept through the village in 1563. The church originally stood at Low Thorpe (the old churchyard is passed on the walk), but in 1810 was replaced by a new church built to mark the golden jubilee of George III and sited by the main road. The village was almost completely rebuilt in the early 1900s, with the houses and gardens occupying exactly the same positions as those shown on an estate map of 1627. The area was once noted for its quarries, and for its grindstones which were hewn on Witton Fell.

Sartorially elegant gent on duty in the last field of the walk.

15 THE HEART OF WHARFEDALE — 6¾ MILES

P Grassington. National Park Centre, Hebden Road. Large car park (pay and display) and toilets. Grid ref: 002 637

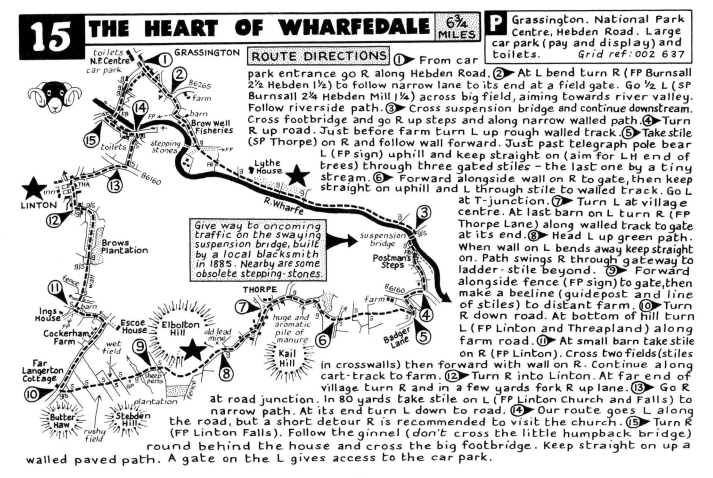

ROUTE DIRECTIONS ① From car park entrance go R along Hebden Road. ② At L bend turn R (FP Burnsall 2½ Hebden 1½) to follow narrow lane to its end at a field gate. Go ½ L (SP Burnsall 2¼ Hebden Mill 1¼) across big field, aiming towards river valley. Follow riverside path. ③ Cross suspension bridge and continue downstream. Cross footbridge and go R up steps and along narrow walled path. ④ Turn R up road. Just before farm turn L up rough walled track. ⑤ Take stile (SP Thorpe) on R and follow wall forward. Just past telegraph pole bear L (FP sign) uphill and keep straight on (aim for LH end of trees) through three gated stiles – the last one by a tiny stream. ⑥ Forward alongside wall on R to gate, then keep straight on uphill and L through stile to walled track. Go L at T-junction. ⑦ Turn L at village centre. At last barn on L turn R (FP Thorpe Lane) along walled track to gate at its end. ⑧ Head L up green path. When wall on L bends away keep straight on. Path swings R through gateway to ladder-stile beyond. ⑨ Forward alongside fence (FP sign) to gate, then make a beeline (guidepost and line of stiles) to distant farm. ⑩ Turn R down road. At bottom of hill turn L (FP Linton and Threapland) along farm road. ⑪ At small barn take stile on R (FP Linton). Cross two fields (stiles in crosswalls) then forward with wall on R. Continue along cart-track to farm. ⑫ Turn R into Linton. At far end of village turn R and in a few yards fork R up lane. ⑬ Go R at road junction. In 80 yards take stile on L (FP Linton Church and Falls) to narrow path. At its end turn L down to road. ⑭ Our route goes L along the road, but a short detour R is recommended to visit the church. ⑮ Turn R (FP Linton Falls). Follow the ginnel (*don't cross the little humpback bridge*) round behind the house and cross the big footbridge. Keep straight on up a walled paved path. A gate on the L gives access to the car park.

Give way to oncoming traffic on the swaying suspension bridge, built by a local blacksmith in 1885. Nearby are some obsolete stepping-stones.

THERE IS BEAUTY AND INTEREST EVERY STEP OF THE WAY ALONG THIS MARVELLOUS WALK. HIGHLIGHTS INCLUDE A 1¼ MILE SECTION OF THE DALES' LOVELIEST RIVERSIDE PATH, A REMARKABLE SUSPENSION BRIDGE, A 'SECRET' HAMLET HIDDEN AMONGST REEF KNOLLS, A VILLAGE FAMED FOR ITS PICTURE - POSTCARD CHARM, IMPRESSIVE WATERFALLS AND A CHURCH IN AN EXQUISITE SETTING. THE ROUTE IS WELL WAYMARKED AND THE GOING IS EASY, WITH NO STEEP GRADIENTS. 1¼ MILES ON MOTOR-ROADS. 3 LADDER-STILES (1 WITH ADJACENT GATE).

15

MAP A

THORPE

This delightfully mellow old hamlet, which once had a thriving boot- and shoe-making industry, is so well hidden among the hills that it was one of the few places to escape the ravages of marauding Scots in the Middle Ages. The handsome Georgian manor house was gutted by fire on the 13th October 1939, but has since been restored to its former glory.

REEF KNOLLS

are smooth, rounded hills of almost pure limestone. Some 300 million years ago, during the geological era known as the Carboniferous period, this area lay submerged beneath a shallow sea. Skeletons and shells of myriads of dead sea-creatures were swept by water currents into submarine ridges. In later geological times earth movements lifted these mounds of limestone above the level of the sea.

THE CAVES OF ELBOLTON HILL

1. NAVVY NOODLE HOLE (ELBOLTON CAVE): Cave entrance at base of small scar. Has yielded remains of prehistoric man and bones of animals which disappeared from Britain thousands of years ago. 2. SHEEP CAVE: Entrance in shakehole. Short passage opens into a chamber. 3. ELBOLTON POT: Entrance pitch concealed in mined passage. An extensive cave system descending to a depth of 135'. 4. ELBOLTON HOLE WEST: Fenced mine shaft dropping into a natural cave. 5. CARVER'S CAVE: Entrance in large shakehole near wall. 6. ESCOE HOUSE HOLE: Large open shaft near wall.

NOTE: There are no rights-of-way on Elbolton's upper slopes. If you intend to mooch about looking for caves, then permission must be sought at Holly Tree Farm, which is passed on the way through Thorpe.

THINGS TO SEE IN AND AROUND LINTON

● VILLAGE GREEN, with its three bridges. The ancient clapper bridge originally stood further downstream, and was moved to its present site when the road bridge was built in 1892. The 14th C. packhorse bridge had parapets added in the 17th C. ● FOUNTAINE'S HOSPITAL (Almshouses). Built in 1721 by Richard Fountaine, a wealthy timber merchant. Chapel in central block open to public. ● FOUNTAINE INN. 17th C. pub with many cosy nooks and crannies. ● CHURCH (St. Michael and All Angels). Built c 1150. Some original Norman fabric. Squat bell-tower possibly 13th C. ● LI'LE EMILY'S BRIDGE (near point ⑮). Tiny humpback bridge named after Emily Norton, a local girl featured in Wordsworth's poem 'The White Doe of Rylstone'. ● FALLS Partly artificial. Adjacent building was cotton-spinning mill until the 1950s.

old guidestone at point ⑬

IN VIEW DIRECTLY AHEAD ON THE APPROACH TO FAR LANGERTON IS THE MONSTROUSLY UGLY SWINDEN QUARRY – THE WORST EYESORE IN THE DALES.

16 THE ASCENT OF LITTLE WHERNSIDE

8½ MILES

P Scar House Reservoir, reached by a highly scenic Water Authority road from Lofthouse. Car park, toilets. Grid ref: 070 766

ROUTE DIRECTIONS ① Cross reservoir dam and fork L up wide stony track. Ignore a track (Nidderdale Way) branching R. ② At T-junction of tracks turn R to climb broad track to gate in ridge-fence. ③ Don't go through gate. Turn L to follow fence/wall/fence to summit (small cairn on other side of fence). ④ Continue alongside fence/wall to descend to a wide saddle. About 200yds beyond its lowest point you will reach an iron post by the wall. ⑤ Turn sharp L (due E). There is no path, but you should be able to spot a marker-post and a narrow path beyond it. You will be heading towards the valley beyond the reservoirs. ⑥ The thin path is followed along the hillside for just over 2 miles, always on a level or very slightly descending course. It is sketchy and boggy, and occasionally disappears altogether. If in doubt maintain a level course. Eventually, by careful navigation or pure chance, and after a lot of swearing, you will return to point ②. Retrace the outward route.

The path along the ridge is shown on the map as a straight line, but in practice you will find yourself on a meandering course around innumerable bogs and peat groughs.

FP Braidley 1½

fence

fence posts

LITTLE WHERNSIDE 1984'

fence

wall

soggy

pools, bogs and peat hags

fence

boggy

fence

Shaw Gill

steep

wall

Trows Beck

Lodge (extensive ruins)

ruin

Carle Fell Side

Carle Fell Road

ruin

rest house

FP

Nidderdale Way

Scar House

broken wall

wall

wall

Wench Gill

sheepfolds

Scar House Reservoir

R. Nidd

car park, toilets, picnic area

A

wall

Hard Bank

wall

B

ravine

Crook Dike

gateway

Angram Pasture

A

wall

B

ravine

⑤ iron post

⑥

x MP

ravine

Great Whernside

* Virtually all the uphill toil occurs between points ② and ④ – 785' of ascent.

Angram Reservoir

A GROUGH is a sheer-sided, foul-smelling, slimy black ditch winding through a quagmire of sodden peat.

42

QUITE STRENUOUS AND NOT TO BE UNDERTAKEN LIGHTLY. EXPECT THE GOING TO BE SOGGY AT THE BEST OF TIMES, AND EXTREMELY BOGGY IN WINTER OR AFTER HEAVY RAIN. IN **MIST** THE ROUTE IS SAFE AS FAR AS THE SUMMIT (POINT ④), BUT **RETURN THE SAME WAY**, AS THE DESCENT ACROSS THE VAST EXPANSE OF ANGRAM MOOR (POINTS ⑤-②) COULD BE A NIGHTMARE. THE WALK'S SAVING GRACE IS THAT IT OFFERS SOME BEAUTIFUL AND UNUSUAL VIEWS. NO LADDER-STILES. NO MOTOR-ROADS.

Though the head of Nidderdale is one of the author's favourite places, this, to be honest, is not exactly his favourite walk. It is included for the benefit of those who take a perverse pleasure in bog-trotting through primeval gunge.

MAP D

THE RESERVOIRS

The building of **SCAR HOUSE DAM** – a colossal engineering project – began in 1921 and was completed in 1936, at which time the spectacular 150' high structure was the biggest dam in the country, and had cost £2·2 million. The access road up which you have driven is built on the line of the Nidd Valley Light Railway, which linked the site to Pateley Bridge. Just before reaching the car park you will see evidence of the village which existed here during the construction years. At the peak of activity the work employed 800 men and the village population was 1,250. The older **ANGRAM RESERVOIR** (started 1904, completed 1913) lies about 100' higher than Scar House and is only about half its size. Two large farmsteads lie submerged beneath its dark waters. The Tufted Duck (see P63) and the Pochard are waterfowl which may be seen on the reservoirs, particularly during the winter months. The handsome pochard drake (L) has a rich chestnut-coloured head and grey back.

Rest House near the dam.

This tablet near the car park commemorates the 50th Anniversary of the opening of Scar House Reservoir.

LODGE

Now a complete ruin, Lodge is thought to occupy the site of a medieval hunting lodge owned by the de Mowbray family. Some 100 years ago there were three farms here. From Lodge we climb the old Nidderdale to Coverdale packhorse road to the crest of the ridge. Efforts are being made to restore the track's surface, which has been badly damaged by vehicles, but it looks like being a big job.

LITTLE WHERNSIDE

IS THE LOWEST OF THE THREE DALES WHERNSIDES, FAILING BY JUST 16' TO ATTAIN MOUNTAIN STATUS. THE TOP OF THIS LONELY FELL IS A BOGGY EXPANSE OF GROUGHS AND PEAT 'CASTLES'. ATOP ONE OF THESE, ON THE N. SIDE OF THE FENCE, STANDS THE FORLORN AND RATHER FEEBLE CAIRN WHICH PURPORTS TO MARK THE SUMMIT. IT IS PRETTY OBVIOUS, HOWEVER, THAT SEVERAL NEIGHBOURING 'CASTLES' ARE HIGHER THAN THE CHOSEN SPOT. YOU WILL FIND SOLITUDE IN THIS REMOTE AND DESOLATE PLACE, AND YOU MAY PAUSE TO REFLECT UPON THE BEAUTIFUL DALES WALKS YOU *MIGHT* HAVE BEEN DOING HAD YOU NOT BEEN DAFT ENOUGH TO CHOOSE THIS ONE.

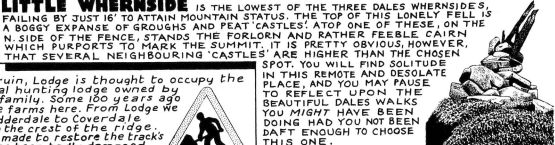

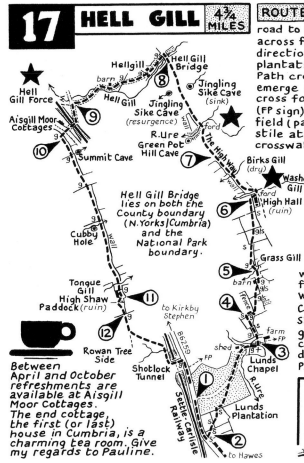

Hellgill

Hell Gill Bridge

barn

Hell Gill Force

★

Hell Gill

Jingling Sike Cave (sink)

Jingling Sike Cave (resurgence)

Aisgill Moor Cottages

Summit Cave

R. Ure

Green Pot Hill Cave

The High Way

★

Birks Gill (dry)

Washer Gill ★

High Hall (ruin)

Hell Gill Bridge lies on both the County boundary (N.Yorks/Cumbria) and the National Park boundary.

Cubby Hole

Grass Gill

barn

Tongue Gill High Shaw Paddock (ruin)

to Kirkby Stephen

fence

Rowan Tree Side

Shotlock Tunnel

B6259

FP

shed

farm → FP

Lunds Chapel

R. Ure

Lunds Plantation

Settle-Carlisle Railway

to Hawes

Between April and October refreshments are available at Aisgill Moor Cottages. The end cottage, the first (or last) house in Cumbria, is a charming tea room. Give my regards to Pauline.

ROUTE DIRECTIONS

① Walk S along road to stile (FP Lunds ½) on L. ② Bear L across field to stile near gate. Maintain direction through two more stiles to enter plantation. Turn R, then L (wm) into trees. Path crosses three small footbridges to emerge onto access drive. Follow it R, cross footbridge and go R through gate (FP sign) to tiny chapel. ③ Take stile/FB to L of chapel (FP sign). Cross field (passing hen huts) to go through gates into walled path. Over stile at its end, then straight across rushy field and over stile in crosswall. ④ Turn R to follow wall. Take gate at corner then sharp L up field to gate/stile in crosswall. Continuing uphill, pass to R of barn (through gate adjoining it) and on past wall-corner to ford small stream. ⑤ Through gate in crosswall and follow wall on R to wall-corner stile/gateway. Keep on climbing diagonally to reach ruins of High Hall. ⑥ At far end of ruin go through gates, then L to ford stream. Follow broad track which soon comes alongside a wall. ⑦ At end of wall keep straight ahead on a level course. ⑧ Cross Hell Gill Bridge, take gate on L and descend farm track. ⑨ At T-junction of tracks turn L (but first go forward ½ R to view waterfall). Cross railway, then road, and up through gate in fence. ⑩ Turn L alongside fence, which soon becomes a wall. When wall turns away keep straight ahead to gate in crosswall. Continue forward, with wall on L all the way to ruins of High Shaw Paddock. ⑪ At far end of ruin bear R through two wall-gaps (old gateways) then forward with wall on L to gate at corner. ⑫ Maintain a level course until you see a path descending L towards the distant parapet of a railway tunnel. Pass behind parapet to gate and turn R along road.

P Lunds Plantation, on the B6259 Garsdale Head - Kirkby Stephen road. It is possible to park here and there on the roadside verges opposite the plantation. Grid ref (plantation entrance): 788 941

THE FAMOUS SETTLE - CARLISLE RAILWAY REACHES ITS SUMMIT JUST SOUTH OF AISGILL MOOR COTTAGES. AT 1169' THIS IS THE HIGHEST POINT ON ANY MAIN LINE IN BRITAIN.

AN INVIGORATING WALK IN THE WILD AND LONELY UPPER RECESSES OF WENSLEYDALE AND THE EDEN VALLEY. THE TERRAIN MAY SEEM BLEAK AND INHOSPITABLE, BUT THERE ARE MANY HIGHLIGHTS ALONG THE WAY, NOT LEAST OF WHICH IS A DRAMATIC GORGE OF AWESOME DEPTH. PATHLESS PASTURES BETWEEN LUNDS CHAPEL AND HIGH HALL INVOLVE A CLIMB OF 350', BUT THE GRADIENT IS GENTLE AND THE REST OF THE WALK IS A DODDLE. NO LADDER-STILES AND ONLY 700 YDS OF MOTOR-ROAD WALKING. SAFE IN MIST, BUT FORDING WASHER GILL AND THE INFANT URE COULD BE AWKWARD IF THE STREAMS ARE IN FULL SPATE.

17

MAP B

LUNDS CHAPEL

HELL GILL is a remarkably deep and narrow ravine which can only be well-seen by those tall enough to peer over the parapet of the sturdy bridge. At **HELL GILL FORCE** the beck, which is soon to become the R.Eden, plunges 60' over a limestone cliff – very impressive when in spate. The R.Ure and Hell Gill Beck are crossed within a distance of 700 yds, yet their points of entry into the sea (Humber Estuary and Solway Firth respectively) are 150 miles apart.

unusual rock formation, lower end of Ure gorge

This tiny, barn-like building, now redundant, was established c 1600 as a chapel-of-ease when the huge medieval parish of Aysgarth was divided into more convenient parts.

THE HIGH WAY Between High Hall and Hell Gill Bridge we walk a section of the coach road used in the late 17th C. by Lady Anne Clifford in travelling from her castle in Skipton to her Westmorland Estates. A century earlier, in 1568, Mary Queen of Scots was taken along the High Way to Bolton Castle, where she was held prisoner.

Mary Queen of Scots

THE CAVES

GREEN POT HILL CAVE is a small resurgence on the south side of the Ure gorge. Difficult to locate and hardly worth the bother. As you approach Hell Gill Bridge look for an obvious valley on the right. At its foot a small stream sinks into JINGLING SIKE CAVE. Retrace your steps to cross the path. The stream re-appears at the foot of a small scar above a rushy depression. The subterranean through trip, a desperate 330 yd journey involving flat-out crawling through mud and slime, can be accomplished by cavers with masochistic tendencies. SUMMIT CAVE (named after the railway summit) is a resurgence in the middle of a field. CUBBY HOLE is a small cave in the S bank of a tiny stream.

Shotlock Tunnel (south entrance)

Built 1875. 106 yds long

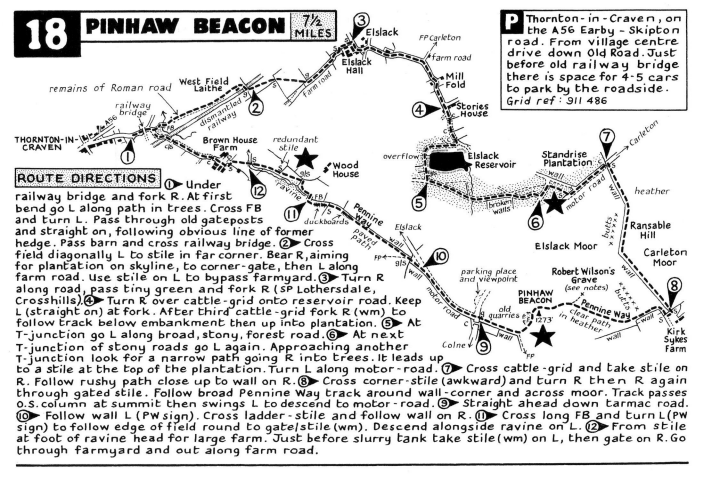

18 PINHAW BEACON 7½ MILES

remains of Roman road · West Field Laithe · Elslack · Elslack Hall · FP Carleton · farm road · Mill Fold · railway bridge · dismantled railway · A56 · THORNTON-IN-CRAVEN · Brown House Farm · redundant stile · Wood House · Stories House · Elslack Reservoir · overflow · Standrise Plantation · Carleton · heather · Ransable Hill · Carleton Moor · Elslack Moor · Robert Wilson's Grave (see notes) · Elslack · Pennine Way · paved path · parking place and viewpoint · PINHAW BEACON · old quarries · 1273' · Pennine Way clear path in heather · Kirk Sykes Farm · Colne · ravine · duckboards · motor road

P Thornton-in-Craven, on the A56 Earby - Skipton road. From village centre drive down Old Road. Just before old railway bridge there is space for 4-5 cars to park by the roadside. Grid ref: 911 486

ROUTE DIRECTIONS

① Under railway bridge and fork R. At first bend go L along path in trees. Cross FB and turn L. Pass through old gateposts and straight on, following obvious line of former hedge. Pass barn and cross railway bridge. ② Cross field diagonally L to stile in far corner. Bear R, aiming for plantation on skyline, to corner-gate, then L along farm road. Use stile on L to bypass farmyard. ③ Turn R along road, pass tiny green and fork R (SP Lothersdale, Crosshills). ④ Turn R over cattle-grid onto reservoir road. Keep L (straight on) at fork. After third cattle-grid fork R (wm) to follow track below embankment then up into plantation. ⑤ At T-junction go L along broad, stony, forest road. ⑥ At next T-junction of stony roads go L again. Approaching another T-junction look for a narrow path going R into trees. It leads up to a stile at the top of the plantation. Turn L along motor-road. ⑦ Cross cattle-grid and take stile on R. Follow rushy path close up to wall on R. ⑧ Cross corner-stile (awkward) and turn R then R again through gated stile. Follow broad Pennine Way track around wall-corner and across moor. Track passes O.S. column at summit then swings L to descend to motor-road. ⑨ Straight ahead down tarmac road. ⑩ Follow wall L (PW sign). Cross ladder-stile and follow wall on R. ⑪ Cross long FB and turn L (PW sign) to follow edge of field round to gate/stile (wm). Descend alongside ravine on L. ⑫ From stile at foot of ravine head for large farm. Just before slurry tank take stile (wm) on L, then gate on R. Go through farmyard and out along farm road.

A GLORIOUS WALK WHEN THE HEATHER'S IN BLOOM, FOR PINHAW BEACON STANDS PROUDLY ATOP ONE OF THE FINEST HEATHER MOORS IN THE DISTRICT. DESPITE A FEW PATHLESS SECTIONS, THE ROUTE IS EASY TO FOLLOW, SAFE IN MIST, AND HAS NO STEEP GRADIENTS, THOUGH THERE IS A STEADY CLIMB OF ABOUT 950' FROM ELSLACK TO THE SUMMIT. 1¼ MILES ON QUIET MOTOR-ROADS. THERE ARE ONLY TWO LADDER-STILES, BUT A FENCE-STILE AND A WALL-STILE AWAIT YOU WITH EVIL INTENT. THE FORMER, JUST BEYOND POINT ⑥, HAS COAT-RIPPING SPIKES OF BARBED WIRE. THE LATTER, AT POINT ⑧, IS AN AWKWARD LITTLE B*!!*! WHERE YOUR BELOVED AUTHOR ONCE NEARLY BROKE HIS NECK.

18

MAP C

cottage and mounting-block   Elslack

ELSLACK is a tiny hamlet consisting of an ancient hall—parts of which date from the 14th C—and a few attractive cottages overlooking a miniature triangular green on which stands an unusual horse-mounting block. 400 yds to the NW of Elslack lie the scant remains of a Roman fort, bisected by the now defunct Skipton-Colne railway. A detour L of ⅓ mile from point ③ will enable you to sample the delights of the excellent Tempest Arms, named after the eminent local family of nearby Broughton Hall.

● ● ●

The dreary **ELSLACK RESERVOIR** was constructed in 1931. It has a surface area of 10 acres.

PINHAW BEACON

The summit, marked by an O.S. column and an untidy cairn, lies at the W end of a long ridge and is where Pennine Way pilgrims, plodding up from Lothersdale, get their first view of true Dales country. Pinhaw, being the highest ground within a wide area, is a wonderful vantage point. To the N are the gleaming limestone scars of Malham; beyond, and a little further W, are the unmistakable profiles of Penyghent and Ingleborough, whilst on very clear days the distant Lakeland peaks are visible to the NW. Closer at hand are dear old Pendle (W) and the dark crags of Barden Moor (NE). Pinhaw was one of a chain of beacons used to relay messages of major significance. In the early 19th C. the beacon had six guards – two each from Lothersdale, Carleton and Elslack. Each pair manned the beacon for a week at a spell, and a hut was provided for them to live in. In 1805 one of the guards, Robert Wilson, was found lying dead in the snow at a spot now marked with an inscribed stone. Just before the Pennine Way track begins to bear L for its final rise to the summit, a prominent green path goes off sharp R. Follow it for about 150 yds to locate the stone.

This stile near Kirk Sykes Farm marks the point at which our route joins the Pennine Way.

Here was found dead The body of Robert Wilson one of The Beacon Gards who Died Jan 29 1805 Aged 59 years

| A SHORT STROLL OVER PINHAW | 3 miles | Park at |

the 'parking place and viewpoint' near point ⑨. This is at the highest point of the Carleton-Colne road (Grid ref: 939 472). Walk NE along the unfenced motor-road for just under a mile to join the described route at point ⑦.

19 MAJESTIC INGLEBOROUGH 8½ MILES

ROUTE DIRECTIONS

① From car park entrance turn R. Pass church, cross bridge and turn R (SP Ingleborough Cave). ② Go R through gate, pay at machine and follow arrows to broad track up Clapdale. ③ Cross wall on L at double ladder-stile and continue along broad path. ④ Path forks. L branch is start of highly prominent path up fellside. To visit fenced crater of Gaping Gill fork R. Circumnavigate crater then head for the steep fellside path. Eventually a flight of stone steps is reached, leading up to an area of cairns and wind-shelters on the 'nose' of Little Ingleborough. ⑤ Continue up the broad path (easier now). On reaching summit plateau turn L (W) to O.S. column and cruciform wind-shelter. ⑥ Return to the wind-shelters at point ⑤. Take a compass bearing almost due south (186°). You will see a shallow but obvious valley (Cote Gill). Make a beeline for it down the pathless fellside. (Note: The line of the right-of-way shown on the O.S. map is a little further W (200°) on higher ground, but in descent it is difficult to pinpoint and follow). ⑦ Follow the shallow valley to a large 'recess' in a crosswall. There's a ladder-stile at its bottom RH corner. Descend walled track, cross road and along lane (SP Newby ½). ⑧ Just before

P Clapham. Large car park (pay and display) and toilets behind the National Park Centre. Grid ref: 745 693 Have some change with you when you set off. There is a small fee (40p at the time of writing) to be paid into a ticket machine at point ②.

INGLEBOROUGH 2372'

Little Ingleborough — many cairns and wind shelters steps

hard work

Fell Beck

Disappointment Pot — Gaping Gill

Flood Entrance Pot

Bar Pot

shakeholes

Beck Head Stream Cave
Clapham Beck Head
Ingleborough Cave
gls
Clapham Beck
FB

small plantation prominent ahead during descent. Keep well to its R.

grotto

Clapdale Wood

FB

Clapdale

FB
FB

The Lake

Ingleborough Hall
car park, toilets

CLAPHAM

From Little Ingleborough the descent to Newby appears somewhat daunting, but there should be no difficulty, though it can be a bit soggy in wet weather. In MIST, however, it's a totally different kettle of fish — DON'T EVEN THINK ABOUT IT.

Cote Gill shallow valley

cave gls
Trow Gill
Foxholes

shaft
stony path
wall

wall
kiln x
shallow valley
quarry
Newby Cote
Clapham—quick return by road
water store
Laithbutts Lane
Newby
Laithbutts
wall

48

VERY STRENUOUS, WITH OVER 1800' OF CLIMBING. THE ASCENT FROM CLAPHAM IS A CLASSIC, WITH A SUCCESSION OF BEAUTIFUL AND AWE-INSPIRING HIGHLIGHTS. VERY CLEAR PATH TO THE SUMMIT PLATEAU, BUT IN MIST, OR SEVERE WINTRY CONDITIONS, IT WOULD BE WISE TO TURN BACK AT GAPING GILL AND COME AGAIN ANOTHER DAY (A POSTPONEMENT BEING PREFERABLE TO A POST MORTEM). THE PATHLESS DESCENT TO NEWBY COTE SHOULD NOT BE ATTEMPTED IN MIST. TWO LADDER-STILES AND ONLY ½ MILE ON (QUIET) MOTOR-ROADS. TAKE A COMPASS AND SOME SPARE WARM CLOTHING – EVEN ON A HOT SUMMER'S DAY IT CAN BE BITTERLY COLD AT THE SUMMIT.

village turn L (BW sign) to gate and path between wall and fence. The path has blue waymarks and is enclosed for almost all its length. ⑨▶ Turn R along road. Fork L to tread carefully along Eggshell Lane.

CLAPHAM

is one of the Dales' prettiest villages, and is a wonderful place to visit. The National Park Centre (dated 1701) is the old Manor House. The market cross (charter granted 1201) is a modern shaft in an ancient base. The lofty and spacious church retains a splendid Perpendicular tower but was otherwise rebuilt in 1814. The ends of ancient pews panel the walls.

One man (Yours truly) and his dog at the summit.

Clapham Church

New Inn

HIGHLIGHTS OF THE ASCENT

● **THE LAKE**: Constructed c1833. Holds about 15 million gallons. ● **INGLEBOROUGH CAVE**: Famous showcave open to the public since 1838. Link with Gaping Gill established 1983. ● **CLAPHAM BECK HEAD**: Major resurgence of water from Gaping Gill system. ● **FOXHOLES**: Large cave entrance not visible from track. A path goes L to it just before track bends L. Has yielded evidence of Neolithic occupation. ● **TROW GILL**: Spectacular dry gorge with 100' high walls. ● **GAPING GILL**: Awesome surface rift where stream plunges 340' down vertical shaft into gigantic chamber. Winch rigged each Bank Holiday to lower visitors (Free, but charge to come back up). An unforgettable experience. *DO NOT APPROACH EDGE OF SHAFT – A SLIP WILL MEAN CERTAIN DEATH.*

INGLEBOROUGH

was once thought to be the highest mountain in England. The huge summit plateau was an ancient hill-fort (sections of its 13' thick perimeter walls still remain). The cruciform wind-shelter incorporates a view indicator, and a nearby pile of rubble is all that remains of a hospice tower built 1830 and destroyed soon afterwards.

An inspiring profile – what walker could resist such a challenge?

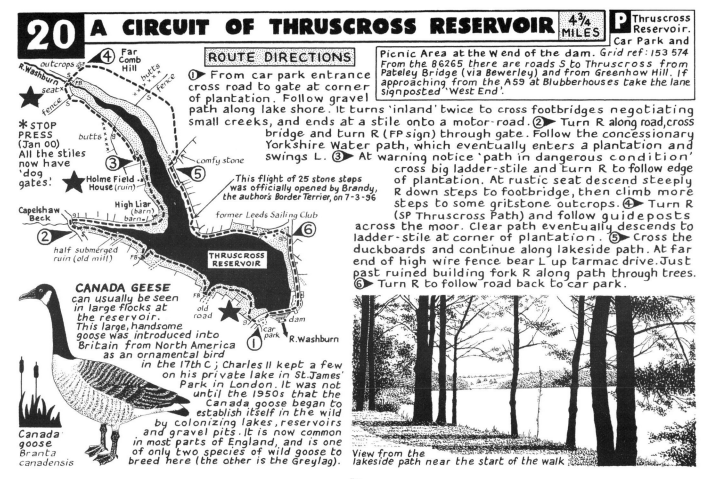

ROUTE DIRECTIONS

① From car park entrance cross road to gate at corner of plantation. Follow gravel path along lake shore. It turns 'inland' twice to cross footbridges negotiating small creeks, and ends at a stile onto a motor-road. ② Turn R along road, cross bridge and turn R (FP sign) through gate. Follow the concessionary Yorkshire Water path, which eventually enters a plantation and swings L. ③ At warning notice 'path in dangerous condition' cross big ladder-stile and turn R to follow edge of plantation. At rustic seat descend steeply R down steps to footbridge, then climb more steps to some gritstone outcrops. ④ Turn R (SP Thruscross Path) and follow guideposts across the moor. Clear path eventually descends to ladder-stile at corner of plantation. ⑤ Cross the duckboards and continue along lakeside path. At far end of high wire fence bear L up tarmac drive. Just past ruined building fork R along path through trees. ⑥ Turn R to follow road back to car park.

Picnic Area at the W end of the dam. Grid ref: 153 574 From the B6265 there are roads S to Thruscross from Pateley Bridge (via Bewerley) and from Greenhow Hill. If approaching from the A59 at Blubberhouses take the lane signposted 'West End'.

*STOP PRESS (Jan 00) All the stiles now have 'dog gates'!

Far Comb Hill

R. Washburn

outcrops

seat

fence

STOP

butts

Holme Field House (ruin)

High Liar (barn)

barn

Capelshaw Beck

half submerged ruin (old mill)

comfy stone

This flight of 25 stone steps was officially opened by Brandy, the author's Border Terrier, on 7-3-96

former Leeds Sailing Club

THRUSCROSS RESERVOIR

old road

car park

R. Washburn

dam

CANADA GEESE
can usually be seen in large flocks at the reservoir. This large, handsome goose was introduced into Britain from North America as an ornamental bird in the 17th C; Charles II kept a few on his private lake in St. James' Park in London. It was not until the 1950s that the Canada goose began to establish itself in the wild by colonizing lakes, reservoirs and gravel pits. It is now common in most parts of England, and is one of only two species of wild goose to breed here (the other is the Greylag).

Canada goose
Branta canadensis

View from the lakeside path near the start of the walk

THIS VERY EASY, AND SUPREMELY BEAUTIFUL, SHORT WALK IN THE LONELY UPPER REACHES OF THE WASHBURN VALLEY IS AN EXQUISITE BLEND OF FOREST TRACKS AND LAKESIDE AND MOORLAND PATHS. THE ROUTE IS ALMOST ENTIRELY ON CONCESSIONARY FOOTPATHS WELL-MAINTAINED BY YORKSHIRE WATER AND AMPLY WAYMARKED; ONLY A GENIUS COULD GET LOST ON THIS ONE. 4 LADDER-STILES (MOST OF THE STILES HAVE ADJACENT GATES WHICH, THOUGH PADLOCKED, CAN BE WRIGGLED UNDER BY SMALL DOGS). ½ MILE ON QUIET MOTOR-ROADS. A PERFECT STROLL FOR A BALMY SUMMER'S EVENING.

The massive dam at Thruscross

THRUSCROSS RESERVOIR is the highest of the four great Washburn reservoirs and was built almost a century after the others. The name 'Thruscross' first appears (as 'Thorescross') in a document of 1299. A hundred feet beneath the lake's dark waters lie the ruins of **WEST END**, a village which, between 1791 and 1889, had mills producing cotton and linen. West End had in effect been doomed since 1897, when Leeds Corporation bought the Thruscross area for waterworks development. The village church (Holy Trinity) was replaced in 1970. Built from the stone of one of the old mills, it cost £25,000 but enjoyed only a brief ecclesiastical life of 16 years before becoming an outdoor pursuits centre. In times of severe drought the ruins of West End resurface, attracting hordes of sightseers and causing such fearful traffic jams that the police have to set up a one-way road system.

THE WASHBURN RESERVOIRS

THRUSCROSS
Completed 1967
Area 142 acres

A 59

FEWSTON
Completed 1879
Area 156 acres

SWINSTY
Completed 1876. Area 156 acres

LINDLEY WOOD
Completed 1875
Area 117 acres

THE CONIFER PLANTATIONS FORM A VALUABLE WILDLIFE HABITAT, PROVIDING FOOD AND COVER FOR BIRDS SUCH AS SISKIN, COAL TIT, GOLDCREST AND REDPOLL. GREY SQUIRRELS ARE MUCH IN EVIDENCE, AND IF YOU'RE VERY LUCKY — AND WALK QUIETLY — YOU MAY CATCH A GLIMPSE OF DEER.

The stile at point ②

HOLME FIELD HEAD, now an atmospheric ruin, was obviously in its heyday a farmhouse of considerable size and consequence. Still intact beneath the crumbling masonry are some splendid barrel-vaulted cellars. According to a local farmer, the house has been unoccupied since about 1910, the last resident being a Mr. John Verity. There may be a family connection with the people named on the rustic memorial seat.

The former **LEEDS SAILING CLUB** has sunk, but not without trace. The forlorn remains include the clubhouse, a small observation hut and a wire fence that would not have looked out of place at Colditz.

The rustic memorial seat

ROUTE DIRECTIONS

① ► Start along road signposted Hetton ½ Gargrave 4. ② ► Pass under railway and immediately turn L along farm road. Go R at fork. Keep L of buildings to follow enclosed bridleway to Hetton. ③ ► Go R through village. ④ ► Fork L (BW Hetton Common) to gate, and continue up broad, walled track. ⑤ ► Turn sharp L along another walled track. ⑥ ► When enclosed track ends at gate, go L with wall towards a barn. Continue forward (tractor trail) alongside wall on L. ⑦ ► Cross tarmac lane to gate (BW Friars Head 1). Follow wall on L. ⑧ ► Turn L (FP Flasby ¾). Bear slightly R, away from wall, and aim for gate high in crosswall in front of small patch of trees. Forward with wall, then fence, on L. Through gate and follow fence down to Flasby. ⑨ ► Cross road and go down lane (SP Flasby). Go L at T-junction. ⑩ ► Pass farm on L then fork L (FP Rylstone 2) up farm road. ⑪ ► Keep R (straight on) at fork. In 80yds turn L (FP sign) and follow fence to rejoin farm road at a barn. ⑫ ► Don't cross cattle-grid. Fork R (FP sign) along cart-track. Just beyond gate ignore a path branching R. ⑬ ► At area of boulders turn L (FP sign) down to gate and cross field to another gate. Pass wall-corner (FP sign) and aim slightly L of railway underpass. Drop to footbridge then climb to underpass. ⑭ ► Climb ½ L. Pass round end of plantation to wall-stile. Forward alongside fence to join cart-track. ⑮ ► Cart-track goes L between walls then turns R. ⑯ ► Turn L at Barn Cottage and R at T-junction.

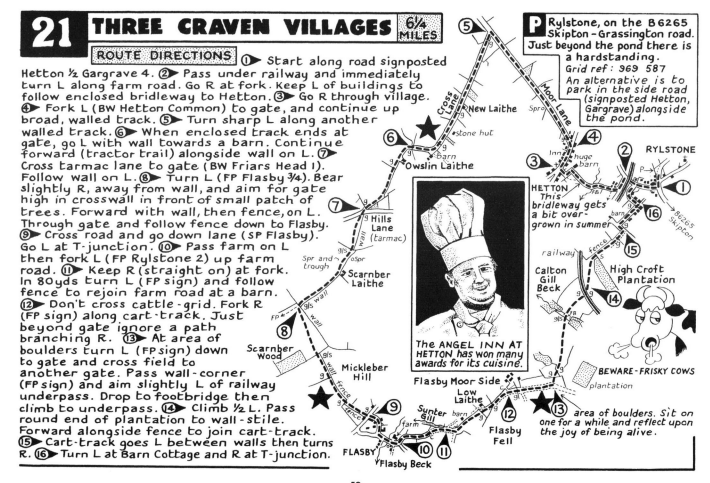

The ANGEL INN AT HETTON has won many awards for its cuisine.

P Rylstone, on the B6265 Skipton – Grassington road. Just beyond the pond there is a hardstanding. Grid ref: 969 587 An alternative is to park in the side road (signposted Hetton, Gargrave) alongside the pond.

Cross Lane
New Laithe
Moor Lane
Spro
stone hut
barn
Owslin Laithe
Inn huge barn
RYLSTONE
HETTON This bridleway gets a bit overgrown in summer
Hills Lane (tarmac)
railway
fence
barn
Skipton B6265
Spr and trough
Scarnber Laithe
wall
Calton Gill Beck
High Croft Plantation
FP
wall
Scarnber Wood
Mickleber Hill
wall fence
fence
BEWARE - FRISKY COWS
plantation
Flasby Moor Side
Low Laithe
Sunter Gill farm
barn
FLASBY
Flasby Beck
Flasby Fell
area of boulders. Sit on one for a while and reflect upon the joy of being alive.

FLOWERY MEADOWS, LUSH PASTURES AND ANCIENT GREEN LANES AND BRIDLEWAYS CHARACTERIZE THIS DELECTABLE RAMBLE LINKING THREE ATTRACTIVE AND HISTORIC LITTLE VILLAGES. PROGRESS IS EASY, WITH NO STEEP GRADIENTS, AND THE VIEWS ARE SURPRISINGLY EXTENSIVE FOR SUCH A LOW-LEVEL WALK. TWO LADDER-STILES (BOTH WITH ADJACENT GATES) AND HALF-A-MILE ON QUIET MOTOR-ROADS. CANINE COMPANIONS WILL PROBABLY HAVE TO BE KEPT, FOR THE MOST PART, ON A LEAD (SHEEP AND COWS ALL OVER THE PLACE).

RYLSTONE

is a pretty village with a history dating back to the Danish Conquest. Its attractive duckpond, bedecked in spring with daffodils, is a familiar landmark to motorists rushing along the B6265. The pond was constructed to power a medieval corn mill which was later, in the 19th C., used as a woollen mill. The Parish Church of St. Peter (not passed on the walk but worth a short detour up the lane opposite the pond) was rebuilt in 1852 around the remains of an early Norman church. Overlooking the church, on the skyline of a colourful gritstone edge, are two more familiar landmarks. Rylstone Cross was erected in 1813 to celebrate the Treaty of Paris, whilst Cracoe Pinnacle – a fine obelisk – commemorates the local dead of World War I. In late 1998 Rylstone emerged from the shadows of obscurity into the glare of national publicity when several members of the local Women's Institute — winsome and comely matrons all — threw aside their inhibitions and their clothes to pose in nature's garb for a quite novel (not to mention titillating) charity calendar.

★ **MOOR LANE** is a broad bridleway climbing gently into the heart of the moors, and offering superb views featuring gritstone edges and conical reef knolls. **CROSS LANE** is a delightful green track between limestone walls.

Owslin Laithe - a typical Dales barn

THE RAILWAY opened in 1902 and ran from Skipton to Threshfield. The single track line now only serves the giant limestone quarry at Swinden, near Cracoe, but at the time of writing (July 99) plans to re-introduce a passenger service are being considered.

HETTON

IS THOUGHT TO HAVE BEEN A SETTLEMENT AS LONG AGO AS THE 7TH C. THIS NEAT, LINEAR VILLAGE HAS SEVERAL COTTAGES AND BARNS SURVIVING FROM THE 1600s. THE WESLEYAN CHAPEL, HETTON'S ONLY PLACE OF WORSHIP, WAS BUILT IN 1859. IN BYGONE DAYS A WEEKLY MARKET WAS HELD IN THE VILLAGE.

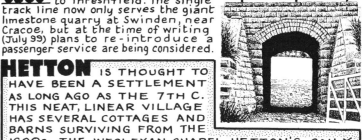

FLASBY, a small farming hamlet, was recorded in the 1086 Domesday Survey as 'Flatebi'. The cottage at point ⑨ displays a doorhead inscribed 'RMO 1683'. Flasby Hall, an Italianate mansion of 1844, now stands in ruins.

★ **FLASBY FELL** is better known by the names of two of its tops — Sharp Haw and Rough Haw. There are two nameless lesser heights.

P Fountains Abbey is well signposted from the A61, B6165 and B6265. Large car parks at the Visitor Centre. Grid ref: 272 686

Horsley Dike
lodge
10
ALDFIELD
13
obelisk
Aldfield Plantation
St. Mary's Church
R. Skell
Spa Ghyll Wood
Low Kirby Wood
ruin
Spa Ghyll Farm
15
R. Skell
FB
Risplith House
R. Skell
11
12
14
1
CP
Visitor Centre
CP
FOUNTAINS ABBEY
farm road
Hind House Farm
ignore stile
hedge
9
8
7
Skell Bank Wood
3
gls
R. Skell
bridge
water treatment works
Low Gate Lane
FB
4
2
pub
Low Gate Lane
farm
trough
gls
Monk Wall
SAWLEY
6
holly
5
Scots pines

ROUTE DIRECTIONS

(1) From CP go to roundabout and L along road. Soon you can use a hedged path on R. When road turns R go straight ahead along bridleway. Rejoin road and drop to first bend. (2) Take gate/stile (FP sign) on R and follow cart-track down to river and into plantation. Pass (mercifully!) a log bridge. (3) Turn L (SP Ripon Rowel) to cross FB. Clear path climbs R to gate/stile at top of wood. Turn L up road. (4) Take stile on R (FP sign) and walk alongside plantation. On reaching gate don't use it, but go R (wm) with hedge. (5) When hedge on L ends go straight ahead, aiming towards RH end of line of Scots pines. Pass through stile in hedge and continue in a straight line past the pines and through several stiles and gates (some wm) to reach the road at Sawley. (6) Turn R through village and R along Low Gate Lane. (7) At treatment works go L (FP sign) down rough lane. (8) At its end take RH of two gates and almost immediately cross stile (wm) on R. Turn L to another stile, then bear slightly R across next field to cross stile and forward with hedge on R. (9) Turn L (wm) at field corner. In 30 yds go through gate (wm) in hedge. Turn L alongside hedge then drop R to stile into farm road. Follow it L to its end and go R along road. (10) 100 yds beyond Grantley Hall lodge take gate/stile (FP sign) on R and follow wide forest track to a ruined building. (11) Immediately past ruin turn L into trees. (Note: For a quick, easy return, omitting the Aldfield section, remain on the forest road, which follows the Skell back to point (2).) In a few yards swing R to green path rising gently to stile (wm) at top of plantation. (12) Continue up sunken path. When it peters out swing L up field (towards houses of Aldfield) to gate (wm). Cross next field to small ladder-stile (wm), then up to wrought-iron gate. (13) Follow road R through village and go R at T-junction. (14) Take stile on L (SP Studley Roger). Cross field diagonally to corner stile and go L along cart-track. When it ends keep straight on towards church to reach stile into road. (15) Cross road and turn R onto footpath leading back to Visitor Centre.

■ ■

A RICHLY VARIED WALK THROUGH EXQUISITELY LOVELY COUNTRYSIDE, LINKING ATTRACTIVE VILLAGES AND EXPLORING THE SECLUDED WOODED VALLEY OF THE RIVER SKELL. EASY GOING, WITH VERY LITTLE UPHILL WORK, ON QUIET LANES, PATHLESS PASTURES AND SHADY FOREST TRACKS. 1½ MILES ON MOTOR-ROADS. 1 (SMALL) LADDER-STILE. SOME OF THE FENCE-STILES COULD DO WITH SOME ATTENTION. FOR A MEMORABLE FAMILY-DAY-OUT COMBINE THE WALK WITH A VISIT TO ONE OF THE COUNTRY'S GRANDEST AND MOST ATMOSPHERIC MONASTIC RUINS.

22

MAP E

Fountains Abbey

Founded c 1132, Fountains grew to become one of the biggest and richest monasteries in the land. It is regarded as probably the most outstanding Cistercian monastic ruin in existence. The abbey, with its Visitor Centre, shop and restaurant, is run by the National Trust and opens daily (except on Fridays in Nov., Dec. and Jan) at 10 a.m.

ALDFIELD

has a history going back possibly some 4,000 years; various discoveries of flints, scrapers and arrow-heads suggest that there was a settlement here in the Stone Age. Don't go charging through the village without visiting the church – it's a little gem. The sundial above the door is dated 1696, but there has been a church here since the 13th C. The present church (c 1782) has a most unusual chapel-like interior, with typically 18th C. three-decker pulpit and box pews.

St. Lawrence the Martyr, Aldfield

Laurence (original spelling), was a Roman Deacon martyred in AD 258

the porch, Sawley Church

two Sawley Arms regulars

SAWLEY

has strong links with Fountains. Marmaduke Huby, the most famous of all Fountains' abbots, built Sawley church at the end of the 15th C. The church was rebuilt in 1769 and again a century later. The Sawley Arms is a popular hostelry noted for fine food.

SPA GILL HOUSE, the ruin at point ⑪, was last occupied in 1957. It was built to provide accommodation for the large numbers of visitors who were coming here in the early 19th C. to sample the waters of Aldfield Spa, a nearby sulphur spring.

ST. MARY'S CHURCH

THIS ECCLESIASTICAL MASTERPIECE WAS BUILT IN 1871 FOR THE MARCHIONESS OF RIPON, IN MEMORY OF HER BROTHER. THE EXTRAVAGANTLY ORNATE INTERIOR IS UNSURPASSED FOR RICHNESS BY ANY CHURCH OF ITS SIZE IN ENGLAND. THE NEARBY **OBELISK** WAS BUILT IN 1805 IN MEMORY OF JOHN AISLABIE, WHO LAID OUT STUDLEY'S SPECTACULAR WATER GARDENS IN THE 18TH C.

5½ MILES

P Bainbridge. Roadside parking spaces in the village.

Be sure not to cause any obstruction or inconvenience to residents. Grid ref: 933 901

ROUTE DIRECTIONS

① Start along the A684 Aysgarth, Leyburn road. ② Just before junction with side-road (Stalling Busk) take stile on R (FP Semerwater 2) and ascend LH side of field. Signposted path passes L of walled enclosure and climbs to crosswall with two adjacent stiles. ③ Take RH stile. In 50yds veer R to walk along crest of hill, then descend, aiming slightly to L of Semerwater, to stile at end of wall. Continue forward through line of stiles. At ladder-stile go R (FP sign) to follow riverbank to Semerwater Bridge. ④ Turn R up steep road. ⑤ At T-junction turn R (Bainbridge 2). In a few yards turn L (FP Hawes End ½) down drive. At first building take gate (wm) on L and climb to barn. Go through its adjoining gate and climb to another barn. There's a wall-stile just above it. ⑥ Climb towards a shallow depression near a wall. Above it is a stile in a crosswall. Follow wall on L up to gate onto road. ⑦ Go R along road to stile on R (FP Hopton Gill Bridge ½). Bear L, crossing ruined wall to descend thin path to white-gated stile. Turn R to follow walled track for 1¼ miles to junction with tarmac road. ⑧ If you're in a desperate rush you could keep straight on here, to follow the road down to Bainbridge. For a more interesting finish turn sharp R up road. ⑨ At RH bend go L into drive (FP Bainbridge ¾). Go straight ahead through wooden gate and ten paces beyond it take stile (FP Bainbridge) on L. Descend ½ R towards wooded ravine. Cross depression and broken wall, then bear slightly L up to gated stile. ⑩ Heading again towards wooded ravine, pass to R of barn then R of wall-corner. Path comes alongside wall on L. Follow it down to Bainbridge.

FOR SOME NOTES ON THE ROMAN ROAD, PLEASE REFER TO PAGE 19 (WALK 4).

Roman Fort

BAINBRIDGE

seat

A684

look back for view of fort

quick return to Bainbridge

barn

barn

FP tarmac road

stone hut

Bainbridge Low Pasture

Cam High Road

Priest Bank

ROMAN ROAD

Bainbridge High Pasture

Gill Edge

Bracken Hill

mast

wall

wall

road

Dales walker c 80 AD

FP

ruined wall

rushes

Hawes End

wall

water lilies

R. Bain

wall

FB

barn

COUNTERSETT

barn

R. Bain

BW Blean Lane

Semerwater Bridge

SEMERWATER

■ ■

A VISIT TO ONE OF THE LOVELIEST PLACES IN THE YORKSHIRE DALES, STARTING FROM ONE OF WENSLEYDALE'S MOST ATTRACTIVE VILLAGES. VERY EASY GOING EXCEPT FOR THE MIDDLE SECTION, WHICH CALLS FOR A CLIMB – STEEP IN PLACES – OF OVER 500' FROM SEMERWATER TO HAWES END. THE WALK IS PREDOMINANTLY THROUGH PASTURES, BUT INCLUDES AN EXHILARATING 1¼ MILE MARCH ALONG AN ANCIENT, ARROW-STRAIGHT HIGHROAD. 1 LADDER-STILE (WITH ADJACENT GATE). ½ MILE ON MOTOR-ROADS. FROM COUNTERSETT THERE IS A SUPERB VIEW OF SEMERWATER, AND FROM HAWES END A QUITE MAGNIFICENT PANORAMA OF WENSLEYDALE.

23

MAP D

BAINBRIDGE

is a village with a very long history. The **ROMANS** came here c 80AD and established a **FORT** on Brough Hill, to the E of the River Bain and at a crossroads on their highway network. The fort was called **VIROSIDUM**, and was occupied for over 300 years. In NORMAN times Bainbridge was the HQ of the Wardens of the **FOREST OF WENSLEY**, a vast hunting tract. Dating from those days is the custom of Bainbridge's famous **FOREST HORN**, which was blown at 9pm every winter's night between Holyrood (14 Sep) and Shrove Tuesday. 3 blasts served to guide benighted travellers to safety. The ceremony is still carried out, whenever possible, and the horn can be seen in the **ROSE AND CROWN**, an excellent hostelry which claims to have been an inn since 1445. The stocks on the green are of uncertain age, but were most probably last used during the reign of Elizabeth the First (1558-1603).

THE BAIN is one of England's shortest rivers, its journey from Semerwater to the Ure being a mere 2 miles. Unlike most rivers, the Bain is sedate in its youth and boisterous in its old age. From Semerwater it meanders lazily through lush meadows, and the reeds and lilies which grow in the still waters at the river's edge provide a perfect habitat for such waterbirds as the moorhen. As it approaches Bainbridge the river gathers momentum to tumble over limestone slabs in a series of fine cascades and waterfalls.

Moorhen

The Carlow Stone

This enormous boulder near the lake shore is reputed to have been a missile hurled by a giant at the Devil.

SEMERWATER

IS THE REMNANT OF A LARGER GLACIAL LAKE FORMED SOME 8,000 YEARS AGO. IT IS STILL A CONSIDERABLE SHEET OF WATER, AND IS A POPULAR VENUE FOR VARIOUS WATER SPORTS. THE LAKE HAS A LEGENDARY 'SUNKEN CITY', THE STORY OF WHICH IS TOLD IN SIR WILLIAM WATSON'S POEM 'BALLAD OF SEMERWATER'. THE LEGEND MAY HAVE A FACTUAL BASIS, FOR THERE IS EVIDENCE THAT THIS WAS THE SITE OF AN IRON AGE LAKE VILLAGE, WHICH COULD HAVE BEEN DESTROYED BY A SUDDEN FLOOD.

George Fox
(1624-1691)

COUNTERSETT

The lovely old hall (1650) was the 17th C. home of Richard Robinson, who established the Quaker faith in Wensleydale. George Fox, founder of the Quakers, stayed here in 1652.

24 HARE HEAD & BOLTON PRIORY 7½ MILES

ROUTE DIRECTIONS

❶ Walk down through village and straight on along road. ❷ Cross main road to gate/stile. Climb to stile near barn, then straight ahead to gate. ❸ Forward along walled green lane into Halton East. Turn R to follow road. ❹ At T-junction cross to gate (FP Broad Park 1¼). Follow wall on L to stile just beyond small wood. Climb to far RH corner of next field (stile) then continue up with wall on R. ❺ At crest of ridge take gate on R and follow broad green track. It eventually descends to run alongside wall. ❻ Track turns R through gate (BW sign) and descends field, crossing a cart-track, to gate in crosswall. Bear L (BW sign) across next field to gate into wood. Follow 'made' path to gate at bottom of wood. ❼ Cross small field to LH of two gates. Forward past ponds then bear R down to gate and cart-track. ❽ Go R along road, then turn L down to Priory. Make your way down to river and follow riverside path downstream. ❾ Keep R of wire fence. When river bends L keep straight on, then follow metal fence R to Devonshire Arms car park. ❿ Turn L along (cont. above R)

ROUTE DIRECTIONS (cont.) road, then, in a few yards, R along lane passing L of the Devonshire Club to gate into walled green path. At its end keep straight on to cross main road via stiles. ⓫ Climb alongside wall on R. ⓬ Through gate (blue arrow) in crosswall. Take level course across field to gate (wm), then straight on, keeping a wall on your L. ⓭ Head towards farmhouse (our route goes along RH side of wall to R of it). Drop to stream and gate, then follow aforementioned wall up to gate. Forward along farm road, which leads back to Draughton.

BW← heather
Middle Hare Head 1004'
High Hare Head
Little Hare Head
rushes
wall
Dog Kennel Plantation
The Old Hall
HALTON EAST
Prior's Bridge
A59
Dutch barn
Embsay and Bolton Abbey Steam Railway
DRAUGHTON
barns
farm road
Haynholme
Banks Gill
pens
fold
Haw Pike ▲ 827'
BCWW N100 AQUEDUCT
inscribed stone
sunken path
dismantled railway
tennis
Devonshire Arms
metal fence
R. Wharfe
Bolton Priory
memorial seat
ponds
Westy Bank Wood
resr
A
Skipton
park here
Ilkley
A65

58

👣 MODERATELY STRENUOUS – NO STEEP GRADIENTS BUT QUITE A LOT OF UPS AND DOWNS. THE EVER-CHANGING TERRAIN INCLUDES PATHLESS PASTURES, HEATHER MOORLAND, VELVETY GREEN BRIDLEWAYS, RIVERSIDE PATHS AND WOODLAND FILLED WITH BIRDSONG. ALLOW PLENTY OF TIME FOR A LEISURELY EXPLORATION OF THE SUPERB PRIORY. I LADDER-STILE. ¾ MILE ON VIRTUALLY TRAFFIC-FREE MOTOR-ROADS. EXQUISITE VIEWS. UNLIKE MANY WALKS AROUND BOLTON ABBEY, THIS ONE IS NOT SUBJECT TO ACCESS AREA RESTRICTIONS, SO BONZO CAN COME WITH YOU.

24

MAP A

former chapel

DRAUGHTON
Pronounced 'Drafton'

A fairly unremarkable village straggling down a hillside between the A65 and the A59. Among the many affluent-looking residences are two old houses of particular appeal – the ancient MANOR HOUSE (1659) and the elegant DRAUGHTON HALL. The remains of the village STOCKS stand close to the tiny ST. AUGUSTINE'S CHURCH (1897), which belongs to the parish of Holy Trinity, Skipton.

At DRAUGHTON BOTTOM you may be lucky enough to see a steam train operating on the EMBSAY and BOLTON ABBEY STEAM RAILWAY. The former Skipton-Ilkley line opened in 1888 and was axed by the infamous Dr. Beeching in 1965. The preserved railway now runs to Bolton Abbey Station, a splendid, newly-constructed replica of the original timber building.

HALTON EAST is a small farming hamlet which dates back to Saxon times. Detour left on reaching its 'main street' to see The Old Hall, a sturdy 17thC house with fine mullions.

An unusual memorial seat in Westy Bank Wood.

William Wordsworth 1770-1850

HARE HEAD

This grassy ridge, though of modest height, provides stunning views of Barden Moor and Wharfedale. The smooth green track along the crest features in Wordsworth's poem 'The White Doe of Rylstone', which tells of a widow, accompanied by her pet deer, regularly trekking over these hills to visit her husband's grave at the Priory. When the widow died, the deer continued to make the journey.

TWO CONTRASTING BUS SHELTERS

Draughton's looks like a pretty garden summerhouse. The one at Halton East resembles a World War pillbox.

Bolton Priory *

The evocative ruins of this once-great monastic house are one of the Dales' prime visitor attractions. Established in 1154 by Augustinians, the Priory, in its heyday, owned land and property far and wide. Much of the Priory was destroyed in 1539, and the fine W tower, begun in 1520, was never to be completed. The nave, however, having been walled off from the rest of the church by Richard Moone, Bolton's last prior, escaped demolition and remains in use as a beautiful Priory Church.

25 COVERDALE 6 MILES

ROUTE DIRECTIONS

P Horsehouse. There is roadside space for 3 or 4 cars at the N end of the village opposite the end of a lane with a 'No Through Road' sign. Grid ref: 047 813

①▶ Go up lane with 'No Through Road' sign. Climb stony path alongside stream to its end at gate/ladder-stile. ②▶ Gently rising path passes old gateposts before climbing alongside wall on R. Approaching wall-corner bear L to skirt boggy area, then climb green path to gate in crosswall at top of field. ③▶ Bear slightly R to follow wall down to plantation. Descend to gate well to R of farm. ④▶ Go L along farm road. Before reaching farm turn R up farm track. ⑤▶ Track ends at big barn. Keep straight on to gate, turn L (FP sign) and follow farm track through another gate (wm). Turn R to follow wall. Before reaching plantation turn L to cross depression and climb to ladder-stile. ⑥▶ Straight on (thin path) along low ridge. After gated stile path veers L to come alongside stream. At another gated stile ford stream and keep straight on (thin path) to eventually enter small field between wall and fence. ⑦▶ At its far end take stile on L then go R alongside wall on R. Keep straight on past house and along farm road. ⑧▶ Straight on along rough lane which soon becomes tarmacked and descends to Carlton. ⑨▶ Turn R down main road. Take gate on L (FP Cover Lane ¼) and go straight down field to stile. Head R to gated stile and forward to road. ⑩▶ Go L down road to stile (FP Gammersgill ¾) on R. Cross stile in wall angle and straight on through another stile and across a small stream. ⑪▶ Keep L of metal gate to wooden gate just beyond. Straight ahead to cross footbridge and enter enclosed path. When it turns R go through stile and bear ½R to stile. Turn L along road into Gammersgill. ⑫▶ At centre of

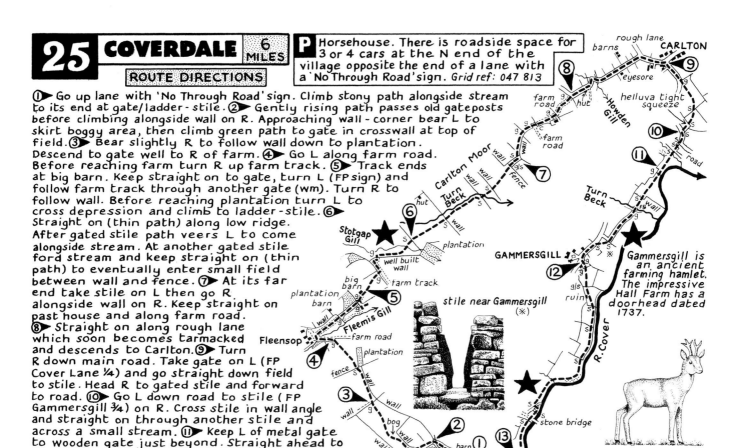

Gammersgill is an ancient farming hamlet. The impressive Hall Farm has a doorhead dated 1737.

stile near Gammersgill (✳)

'Hindlethwaite' means 'forest clearing for hinds' (female deer).

A WALK OF CONTRASTS, WITH LONELY UPLAND PASTURES, RESONANT WITH BIRDSONG, GIVING WAY TO LUSH RIVERSIDE MEADOWS. THE INITIAL CLIMB OF SOME 570' FROM HORSEHOUSE TO POINT ③ (THE HIGHEST POINT OF THE WALK AT 1388') IS FAIRLY STRENUOUS; THEREAFTER THE GOING IS VERY EASY. ONE OF THE HIGHLIGHTS OF THIS CHARMING RAMBLE IS THE SECLUDED VALLEY OF FLEEMIS GILL, A VERDANT AND TRANQUIL PLACE RARELY VISITED BY WALKERS. LOTS OF STILES, BUT ONLY TWO OF THE LADDER VARIETY. ¼ MILE ON QUIET MOTOR-ROADS.

hamlet take gate (FP Swineside ¾) on L and drop to small gate in RH corner. Cross centre of field to gate/stile then down to stile (wm) in far corner. Follow riverbank upstream - there's no path, but the route is obvious through a series of stiles. ⑬▶ Just beyond big footbridge take small gate in crosswall. Bear ½ R up to Horsehouse (route marked by huge, white, wooden arrows).

★ COVERDALE ★

is the longest of Wensleydale's many side-valleys. From its rising on the slopes of Great Whernside the River Cover flows for some 15 miles to join the Ure just below Middleham. A famous son of the dale was Miles Coverdale, Bishop of Exeter, who undertook the first translation of the Bible into English - a task he completed in 1535.

MILES COVERDALE 1488-1568

This old caravan has nestled snugly under its archway at Gammersgill for donkey's years, and has become a familiar landmark for motorists driving up the dale.

HORSEHOUSE

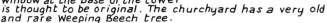

St. Botolph's, Horsehouse

The hoary old grey buildings of this tiny village cluster haphazardly around a cosy pub (Thwaite Arms) and a modest little church. The name 'Horsehouse' suggests that this was a resting-place for packhorses travelling between Wharfedale and Middleham. St. Botolph's Church was established c1530 as a chapel-of-ease run by the monks of Coverham Abbey. It was rebuilt in 1869, but the window at the base of the tower is thought to be original. The churchyard has a very old and rare Weeping Beech tree.

*

ST. BOTOLPH, ACCORDING TO THE ANGLO-SAXON CHRONICLE, WAS THE FOUNDER AND FIRST ABBOT OF A MONASTERY AT ICANHOE IN 654, BUT IT IS UNCERTAIN WHETHER THIS WAS AT IKEN (SUFFOLK) OR BOSTON (LINCS), WHERE THE PARISH CHURCH - THE FAMOUS BOSTON STUMP - IS ONE OF SOME 70 ENGLISH CHURCHES DEDICATED TO THIS RATHER OBSCURE SAINT. ST. BOTOLPH'S DAY IS THE 17TH JUNE.

CARLTON is a very long village, as you will discover should you decide to detour L at point ⑨ in order to wet your whistle at the excellent Foresters Arms. On the way you will pass a house with a prominent tablet stating that this was the home of Henry Constantine (a local dialect poet known as 'The Coverdale Bard').

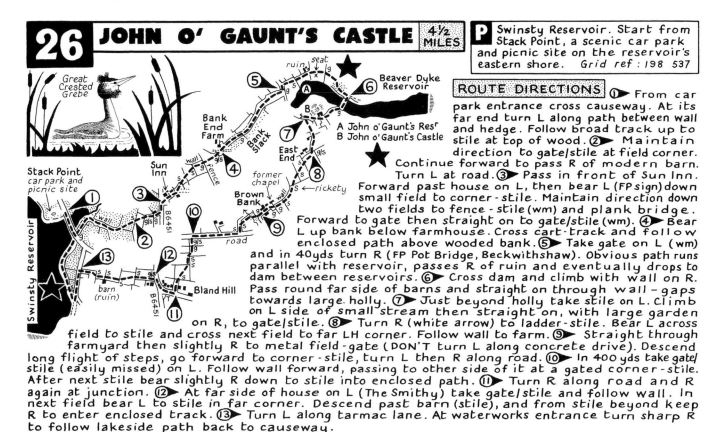

26 JOHN O' GAUNT'S CASTLE

4½ MILES

Great Crested Grebe

Beaver Dyke Reservoir

Bank End Farm

A John o' Gaunt's Resʳ
B John o' Gaunt's Castle

Bank Slack

East End

Sun Inn

former chapel

← rickety

Brown Bank

Stack Point car park and picnic site

B6451

Bland Hill

barn (ruin)

B6451

Swinsty Reservoir

P Swinsty Reservoir. Start from Stack Point, a scenic car park and picnic site on the reservoir's eastern shore. Grid ref: 198 537

ROUTE DIRECTIONS

① From car park entrance cross causeway. At its far end turn L along path between wall and hedge. Follow broad track up to stile at top of wood. ② Maintain direction to gate/stile at field corner. Continue forward to pass R of modern barn. Turn L at road. ③ Pass in front of Sun Inn. Forward past house on L, then bear L (FP sign) down small field to corner-stile. Maintain direction down two fields to fence-stile(wm) and plank bridge. Forward to gate then straight on to gate/stile (wm). ④ Bear L up bank below farmhouse. Cross cart-track and follow enclosed path above wooded bank. ⑤ Take gate on L (wm) and in 40yds turn R (FP Pot Bridge, Beckwithshaw). Obvious path runs parallel with reservoir, passes R of ruin and eventually drops to dam between reservoirs. ⑥ Cross dam and climb with wall on R. Pass round far side of barns and straight on through wall – gaps towards large holly. ⑦ Just beyond holly take stile on L. Climb on L side of small stream then straight on, with large garden on R, to gate/stile. ⑧ Turn R (white arrow) to ladder-stile. Bear L across field to stile and cross next field to far LH corner. Follow wall to farm. ⑨ Straight through farmyard then slightly R to metal field-gate (DON'T turn L along concrete drive). Descend long flight of steps, go forward to corner-stile, turn L then R along road. ⑩ In 400 yds take gate/stile (easily missed) on L. Follow wall forward, passing to other side of it at a gated corner-stile. After next stile bear slightly R down to stile into enclosed path. ⑪ Turn R along road and R again at junction. ⑫ At far side of house on L (The Smithy) take gate/stile and follow wall. In next field bear L to stile in far corner. Descend past barn (stile), and from stile beyond keep R to enter enclosed track. ⑬ Turn L along tarmac lane. At waterworks entrance turn sharp R to follow lakeside path back to causeway.

THE WASHBURN VALLEY is Yorkshire's version of the Lake District, and its lakes, though artificial, can rival Cumbria's natural meres in the beauty of their settings. The area's close proximity to the massive Leeds/Bradford conurbation ensures its tremendous popularity with walkers and anglers.

■ ■ ■ ■ ■ ■ ■ ■ ■ ■ ■ ■ ■ ■ ■ ■ ■ ■ ■ ■

A SHORT AND VERY EASY STROLL IDEAL FOR A BALMY SUMMER'S EVENING (SHOULD WE EVER GET ONE) OR A CRISP WINTER'S DAY. VARIED TERRAIN, INCLUDING LAKESIDE AND WOODLAND PATHS, GREEN TRACKS AND PATHLESS PASTURES. I LADDER - STILE. ½ MILE ON MOTOR - ROADS. COSY PUB EN ROUTE. WHEN THE WALK WAS RESEARCHED (Jan 00) SOME OF THE GATES AND STILES WERE IN A DECREPIT CONDITION. **A SOMEWHAT COMPLEX ROUTE REQUIRING CAREFUL REFERENCE TO MAP AND DIRECTIONS.**

26

MAP F

Tufted Duck

SWINSTY RESERVOIR was completed in 1876 and has
a surface area of 156 acres. (For details of the other Washburn reservoirs see P51). The car park at Stack Point is hugely popular, attracting ramblers, anglers, birdwatchers, picnickers, dog exercisers and duck feeders. Yorkshire Water has considerably provided concessionary paths to enable walkers to enjoy a beautiful circuit of the reservoir (2¾ miles). Birdlife abounds. On and around the water you are likely to see great crested grebe, heron, grey wagtail, tufted duck and goosander. In the plantations look out for jay, coal tit, goldcrest and great spotted and green woodpecker.

★

Ruined farmhouse above John o' Gaunt's Reservoir. A nearby memorial seat makes a perfect picnic place.

THE SUN INN at Norwood is an excellent watering-hole - good food, good ale, good atmosphere and open all day.

HAVERAH PARK was a royal hunting forest from
the late 12th C. By the mid 16th C. the deer had been hunted almost to oblivion, and in 1628 Charles I sold the park to the City of London. The land was acquired by the Ingilbys of nearby Ripley in 1639. JOHN O' GAUNT'S RESERVOIR was constructed in 1800 and is probably the oldest Yorkshire reservoir still in use. BEAVER DYKE RESERVOIR dates from 1890.

At **BANK SLACK** an ancient track follows the line of an earthwork believed to have been constructed by an Iron Age tribe some two thousand years ago.

John o' Gaunt's Castle
was never a castle, but a medieval hunting lodge which is known to have existed as long ago as 1335 - five years before John o' Gaunt was born. John o' Gaunt was the 4th son of Edward III, and his eldest brother was the Black Prince. The Black Prince predeceased Edward, but his son succeeded to the throne in 1377 as Richard II. The new king was but 10 years of age, and his uncle - John o' Gaunt - became the power behind the throne and virtually ruled the country. As Duke of Lancaster and Lord of Knaresborough he was a man of considerable land and property.

27 BARBONDALE 8½ MILES

ROUTE DIRECTIONS

P Barbon. Park at the roadside in the village centre. The best places are by the telephone box or near the church. Be sure to park considerately. *Grid ref (church): 630 824*

① ► Start along tarmac drive (FP sign) at E side of church. Follow it over the beck and up the hillside. ② ► At FP sign fork R off drive along green track to gate into wood. Follow broad track, keeping always on L side of beck, through woodland and then open country for 1¼ miles to a roadside footbridge. ③ ► Turn R along road. Beyond bridge take second track on L (BW Bullpot). Clear, stony path climbs to gate in crosswall and continues as a walled track to reach head of tarmac lane. ④ ► Go L to Bullpot Farm. Take small gate (wm) to L of it, and follow broad path for 200yds to Bull Pot of the Witches. Return to tarmac lane and walk up it for ½ mile. ⑤ ► Before reaching farm (down on your L) go R through gate (FP sign) and climb broad green path to gate in crosswall. Continue on clear path which soon begins a long descent to eventually run alongside a wall. Go through gate and down walled track. ⑥ ► Turn R down tarmac lane. ⑦ ► At a crossroads of lane and tracks turn R (BW Bents Lane) and follow walled track to its end. ⑧ ► Turn R along tarmac road, which soon becomes unenclosed. At road-junction turn sharp L over cattle-grid and follow road back to Barbon.

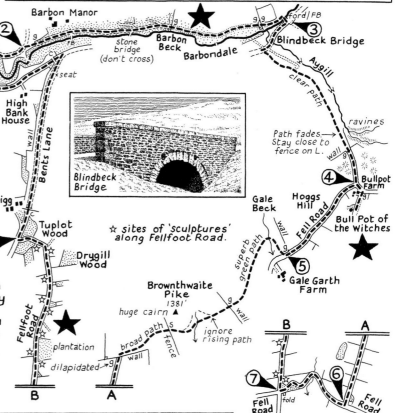

Blindbeck Bridge

☆ sites of 'sculptures' along Fellfoot Road.

Barbon Manor • *Barbon Beck* • *Barbondale* • *ford/FB* • *Blindbeck Bridge* • *Aygill* • *clear path* • *ravines* • *Path fades. Stay close to fence on L.* • *Bullpot Farm* • *Hoggs Hill* • *Bull Pot of the Witches* • *Fell Road* • *Gale Beck* • *superb green path* • *Gale Garth Farm* • *Brownthwaite Pike 1381' huge cairn* • *ignore rising path* • *Fell Road* • *fold* • *Fell Road*

BARBON • *inn* • *seat* • *High Bank House* • *Bents Lane* • *Whelprigg* • *Tuplot Wood* • *Drygill Wood* • *Fellfoot Road* • *plantation* • *dilapidated* • *stone bridge (don't cross)* • *seat* • *wall*

64

AN EXQUISITE WALK OF WONDERFUL VARIETY, INCORPORATING PARKLAND, WOODLAND AND BECKSIDE SCENERY, BLEAK, DESOLATE MOORS AND SUPERB GREEN TRACKS, WITH A VISIT TO A FAMOUS POTHOLE THROWN IN FOR GOOD MEASURE. THERE ARE SEVERAL UPHILL SECTIONS, THE MOST STRENUOUS BEING THAT BETWEEN BLINDBECK BRIDGE AND BULLPOT FARM, BUT THE GRADIENTS ARE NOWHERE PARTICULARLY STEEP. BEING ON GOOD, CLEAR PATHS AND TRACKS THROUGHOUT, THE WALK IS PERFECTLY SAFE IN MIST, BUT IT WOULD BE A PITY TO MISS THE GLORIOUS VIEWS.   NO LADDER-STILES. 1½ MILES ON VERY QUIET MOTOR-ROADS.

lych gate,
Barbon church.

BARBONDALE

There are those who would opine that Barbondale should have no place in a book about the Yorkshire Dales, for it lies neither in Yorkshire nor in the Dales National Park. Nevertheless, it cannot be denied that this lonely and beautiful valley has a definite Yorkshire Dales flavour. Barbondale has been in Cumbria since the tragic demise of the much-lamented Westmorland, one of England's loveliest counties. The narrow road which snakes between the high fells to Dentdale passes through the tiny, unspoiled village of BARBON, where hungry and/or thirsty visitors may seek sustenance at the POST OFFICE and/or the cosy BARBON INN. ST. BARTHOLOMEW'S CHURCH was built in 1893 on the site of much earlier churches. DO take a look inside and note how spick and span and lovingly cared-for it is. Village pride is manifest here.

St. Bartholomew's

BULL POT OF THE WITCHES

is a fearsome, tree-girt, 210' deep open shaft. It is possible (though the author wouldn't dream of doing it) to lean against a tree on the lip of the hole and peer down into its inky depths. Bull Pot is connected to the caverns of EASE GILL, a magnificent cave system containing long, winding streamways, huge waterfall shafts and some of Britain's best stalactite displays. BULLPOT FARM has long been the base of the Red Rose Caving Club.

? As you wander up Fellfoot Road you will notice, on either side of the track, a series of what appear to be small sheepfolds, each containing a single large boulder. These are the work of one Andy Goldsworthy, who is apparently an 'internationally-renowned sculptor'. Quite what they are meant to represent is not obvious to the author (who is admittedly a bit of a Philistine in such matters).

P Airton. Roadside parking is possible by the village green, but be sure not to cause obstruction or inconvenience. Grid ref : 902 591
Alternatively there is space for a few cars at the E end of the village, by the bridge, on the Calton, Winterburn road.

ROUTE DIRECTIONS

① Start along road signposted Otterburn and Hellifield at SW corner of green. ② At end of row of cottages turn L along lane (SP Bell Busk 2). In 250 yds fork R along farm road (Kirk Syke Farm). ③ Keep straight on at farm (don't enter farmyard). ④ Track ends at barn. Keep straight on to gate and follow fence on L to its junction with a wall. Through gate (BW sign) and follow fence down to barn and bridge. Continue forward along cart-track. ⑤ Turn L along road. At road junction cross bridge and immediately fork R (BW sign) to cross another. Continue up lane. ⑥ Track turns L (don't cross cattle-grid). ⑦ When track turns R go straight ahead through gate and up tractor trail. Detour L above quarry to visit Haw Crag, then return to fence and follow it to gate/stile. ⑧ Turn ½ L and pass mid-way between two powerline poles before dropping to ladder-stile hidden in field-corner. Follow wall forward, but when it begins to veer L keep straight on (PW sign) down towards converging walls. ⑨ Follow small stream L to cross footbridge over R. Aire. Follow obvious riverside path upstream to road bridge. ⑩ Cross the bridge and take stile on L (PW sign) to rejoin river bank. Through stile (PW sign) in crosswall and forward alongside wall on R. ⑪ Cross two adjacent stiles then head for stile near powerline pole. Continue upstream, gradually nearing river, to stile at road bridge. Turn L up road into Airton.

WATER BIRDS of many kinds find this quiet stretch of the infant Aire a desirable habitat. Most often espied will be the bobbing and curtseying **DIPPER**, the shy, red-billed **MOORHEN**, the stately **GREY HERON** and, of course, the ubiquitous **MALLARD**. With extreme good fortune you may glimpse a flash of iridescent blue as a **KINGFISHER** speeds along the water. Large flocks of **CANADA GEESE** can often be seen by Otterburn Beck.

Mallard

■ ■

FIND PEACE AND SOLITUDE IN THIS LITTLE-FREQUENTED CORNER OF LOVELY MALHAMDALE. THE WALK IS LEVEL ALMOST THROUGHOUT, THE ONLY EXERTION BEING A GENTLE CLIMB OF 230' FROM BELL BUSK TO THE SUMMIT OF HAW CRAG. PREDOMINANTLY LANES AND FARM TRACKS, WITH AN EXQUISITE FINAL MILE ALONG THE BANKS OF THE YOUTHFUL AIRE. 1 LADDER-STILE (WITH ADJACENT GATE). ½ MILE ON QUIET MOTOR-ROADS. REMARKABLY EXTENSIVE VIEWS.

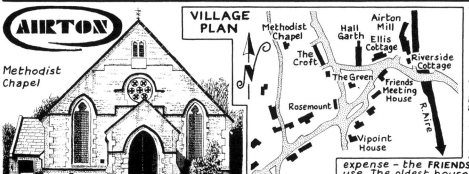

AIRTON

Methodist Chapel

VILLAGE PLAN

Methodist Chapel · Hall Garth · Airton Mill · Ellis Cottage · The Croft · Riverside Cottage · The Green · Friends Meeting House · Rosemount · R. Aire · Vipoint House

This way for ↓ Kirk Syke

This neat and spacious village is largely neglected by tourists, there being no pubs or shops to attract the attention of speeding motorists hell-bent for Malham. Airton's focal point is a large **GREEN**, in the middle of which stands a house known as **SQUATTERS' COTTAGE**. The original house was what is now the garage. Nearby are the remains of the village **STOCKS**. **ELLIS COTTAGE** was built in 1696 by William Ellis, a linen-weaver who became an early convert to the 'Quaker' faith and went on preaching missions to America. Ellis also built – in 1700 and at his own expense – the **FRIENDS' MEETING HOUSE**, which is still in use. The oldest house in Airton is **VIPOINT HOUSE**, built in the year of the Great Fire of London. Just along the Malham road is the **METHODIST CHAPEL** (1896).

BELL BUSK
is a small, scattered hamlet at the confluence of Otterburn Beck and the River Aire. Dominating the scene is the railway, which crosses the Aire on a 7-arch viaduct. The church spire visible beyond is that of St. Peter's, Coniston Cold. So hushed and sleepy is Bell Busk nowadays that it is hard to believe that a century ago there were mills spinning silk here.

★

HAW CRAG,
a grassy hillock of modest elevation, owes its dramatic appearance to the 19th C. quarrymen who gouged out its southern slopes.

stile at Newfield Bridge

SCOWBANK BRIDGE carries the Calton road over the Aire. The small arch was used as an air-raid shelter during World War II. In the background is **AIRTON MILL**, converted into flats in 1972. Built in 1788 as a cotton mill, it was greatly enlarged in 1836 and in 1918 became an engineering works. In 1942 Reckitts purchased the mill and manufactured Dettol. Between 1960 and 1972 the building was used to breed poultry. In front of the mill stands **RIVERSIDE COTTAGE**, which was the mill manager's house.

29 REDMIRE FORCE & THE TEMPLARS' CHAPEL 6¾ MILES

ROUTE DIRECTIONS

①▶ Walk up road towards village. At house on L 'Valley View' fork R down lane then turn R down walled track. Follow enclosed path to its end, at two gates. ②▶ Take RH gate. Follow wall on L, and when it turns away L drop down to LH corner of field to locate gate in wall. ③▶ Cross stream and turn R (SP Hestholme Br) to gate/stile in fence. Follow riverside path upstream. ④▶ Path swings away from river alongside wall and woodland. Cross ladder-stile and straight on across field to small gate at its RH corner. Clear path descends to Redmire Force. ⑤▶ Climb stepped path to small gate. Forward (FP sign) with wall on R. ⑥▶ Keep straight on, now with fence on L. Cross a field-corner via two stiles and continue with wire fence on L. When it turns L head for far RH corner of field. Cross stile and descend to stepping-stones (don't cross them). ⑦▶ Through gate and follow wall on L up to main road. Turn L. ⑧▶ Take small gate on R (FP Templars Chapel ½). Follow track between wall and wire fence up to gate into wood. Climb stony track to wall-stile on L (FP West Witton 1½). ⑨▶

P West Witton, on the main (A684) Wensleydale road. There is a large layby just before entering the village from the east.
Grid ref : 067 885

Forward alongside wall on L. ⑩▶ Cross farm road to gate (FP West Witton 1). Forward alongside wall on L. ⑪▶ Don't use stile onto main road. Instead bear ½ R (FP West Witton ½) up to gap-stile in crosswall. Cross next field to fence-gate, then maintain direction past powerline pole to stile at far RH corner. ⑫▶ Through small plantation (awkward, wet path). Near end of next field go R through wall-stile then L (FP sign). Straight on through two stiles to main road. ⑬▶ Turn R to follow road through West Witton (two good pubs) and back to layby.

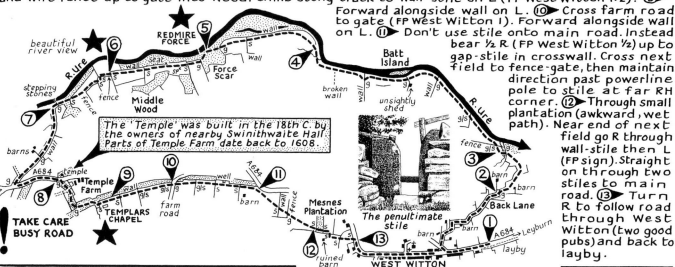

REDMIRE FORCE
★
beautiful river view ★
R. Ure
⑥
⑤
wall
seat
wall
s s s
sp s
g
g
Force Scar
④
Batt Island
broken wall
unsightly shed
R. Ure
fence g/s
③
② barn
barn
Back Lane
stepping stones
⑦ s s fence
fence
Middle Wood

The 'Temple' was built in the 18th C. by the owners of nearby Swinithwaite Hall. Parts of Temple Farm date back to 1608.

barns
g
wall
A684
temple
⑧
Temple Farm
⑨ wall
TEMPLARS CHAPEL
★
! TAKE CARE BUSY ROAD
⑩
g/s
g
farm road
well
A684
g/s
barn
⑪
wall fence
Mesnes Plantation
s s
⑫
s
s
ruined barn
⑬
s
barn
barn
A684 → Leyburn
layby
WEST WITTON

The penultimate stile

■ ■

EASY AND PREDOMINANTLY LEVEL WALKING THROUGH THE RIVERSIDE MEADOWS AND HILLSIDE PASTURES OF AN EXQUISITELY BEAUTIFUL PART OF WENSLEYDALE. THE 2½ MILE SECTION ALONGSIDE THE URE – ONE OF THE FINEST RIVERSIDE WALKS IN THE DALES – IS AN ABSOLUTE RIOT OF COLOUR ON A SUNNY AUTUMN DAY. THE RETURN ROUTE PASSES THE PIQUANT REMAINS OF A TINY MEDIEVAL CHAPEL BUILT BY THE MYSTERIOUS KNIGHTS TEMPLAR. 3 LADDER-STILES AND 1 MILE ON MOTOR-ROADS (MOSTLY WITH GRASS VERGES OR WALKWAYS).

WEST WITTON,

an ancient and attractive village, is perhaps best-known for a quaint old tradition. On the nearest Sunday to St. Bartholomew's Day (Aug 24) villagers chant a rhyme as they march down the street carrying an effigy of 'Owd Bartle', who is then ceremonially burned à la Guy Fawkes. There are conflicting theories as to the origin of Owd Bartle, the most popular claiming that he was a thief who stole swine from Jervaulx Abbey.

REDMIRE FORCE is a series of wide, low waterfalls. Not so well-known as the famous falls at Aysgarth, but nevertheless impressive after heavy rain, and in a beautiful setting. The banks of the Ure hereabouts abound with birdlife; look for sand martin, heron, nuthatch and treecreeper.

Sand Martin

Dark brown with white underparts and a dark throat.

The Rhyme of Owd Bartle

At Penhill Crags
he tore his rags;

At Hunter's Thorn
he blew his horn;

At Capplebank Stee
he brak his knee;

At Grisgill Beck
he brak his neck;

At Wadham's End
he couldn't fend;

At Grass Gills End
they made his end;
Shout, lads, shout.

St. Bartholomew's West Witton

Templars

were members of a military-religious order which was founded in 1118 to protect pilgrims on their way to the Holy Land. Their headquarters were near Solomon's Temple in Jerusalem, and their original and full title was 'Poor Knights of Christ and of the Temple of Solomon.' The order spread throughout much of Europe and became extremely powerful, but was disbanded in the 14th C. The Penhill Preceptory was built c 1200 and handed over to the Knights Hospitallers in 1312. Excavations in 1840 revealed the low ruins of a tiny chapel which was, in all probability, part of a larger establishment which remains hidden.

stone coffin, Templar's Chapel

P Halton Gill. Small car park (honesty box) at entrance to village.
Grid ref: 881 764

ROUTE DIRECTIONS

① Walk through village and take gate on R (FP Beckermonds 2½) to stony track. ② Pass through gate/stile in fence and turn L up green path (FP Beckermonds) to ladder-stile. Follow sunken path by wall. When wall bends L turn R uphill. Cross a sunken track and continue up thin path (wm) to ladder-stile. ③ Straight on along sketchy path which winds gently upwards through limestone outcrops to another ladder-stile. Keep straight on along level, sketchy path. ④ Soon after crossing a stream (FP sign) the path turns uphill to cross a broken wall. Straight on up clear path to ridge-wall ladder-stile. ⑤ Forward past pile of stones and descend towards buildings of Beckermonds at bottom of plantation. ⑥ Through gate and turn R (SP Deepdale, Dalesway) to follow riverside path (wm). ⑦ Cross road-bridge and turn R up drive (Deepdale Farm). At L bend go R through gate (FP Yockenthwaite). Follow clear path to footbridge, keep round L edge of field to ladder-stile, then forward to rejoin river bank. ⑧ At farm turn sharp R to cross bridge, then go L along road. ⑨ Just before buildings turn R (BW Halton Gill). Path goes through small cleft in outcrops, swings R then winds rather vaguely uphill. Stay roughly parallel with gill on L and soon you'll locate a clear, stony track. Follow it over ridge and down to Halton Gill

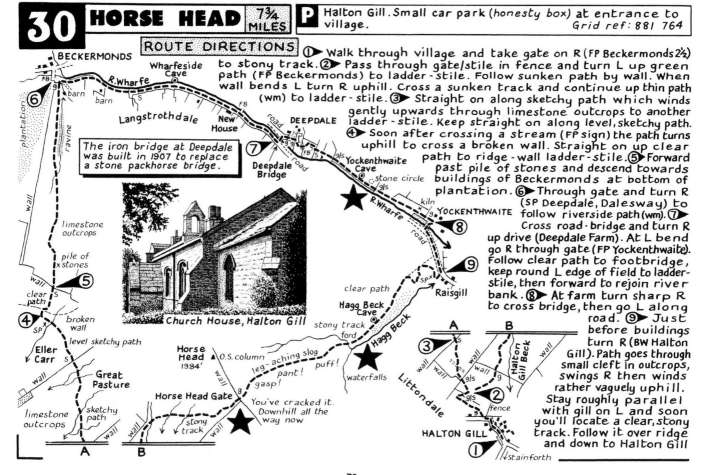

The iron bridge at Deepdale was built in 1907 to replace a stone packhorse bridge.

Church House, Halton Gill

BECKERMONDS
Wharfeside Cave
R. Wharfe
barn barn
plantation
ravine
Langstrothdale
New House
DEEPDALE
road
Deepdale Bridge
Deepdale Cave
Yockenthwaite Cave
stone circle
kiln
R. Wharfe
YOCKENTHWAITE
road
Raisgill
clear path
Hagg Beck Cave
Hagg Beck
stony track
ford
waterfalls
Littondale
Halton Gill Beck
wall
fence
HALTON GILL
Stainforth

limestone outcrops
pile of stones
wall
clear path
broken wall
Eller Carr
level sketchy path
Great Pasture
limestone outcrops
sketchy path
wall
Horse Head 1984'
O.S. column
leg-aching slog pant! puff! gasp!
You've cracked it. Downhill all the way now
Horse Head Gate
stony track
wall

A B

THIS STRENUOUS DOUBLE CROSSING OF THE HIGH RIDGE SEPARATING THE LOVELY VALLEYS OF LITTONDALE AND LANGSTROTHDALE INVOLVES A TOTAL ASCENT OF 1600! THE WALK HAS THREE DISTINCT SECTIONS, VIZ: 1. HALTON GILL TO BECKERMONDS. THE GRADIENTS ARE GENERALLY MODERATE, BUT THE PATH IS NOT WELL-DEFINED, AND BECAUSE OF THIS THE WALK IS *NOT RECOMMENDED IN MIST.* 2. BECKERMONDS TO YOCKENTHWAITE. A 2-MILE AMBLE ALONG ONE OF THE MOST BEAUTIFUL RIVERSIDE WALKS IN THE DALES. 3. YOCKENTHWAITE TO HALTON GILL. CLEAR TRACK, BUT STEEP AND ROUGH UNDERFOOT. 6 LADDER-STILES. ½ MILE ON MOTOR-ROADS. GLORIOUS VIEWS.

30

MAP D

HALTON GILL

is a tiny, haphazard cluster of grey buildings mostly dating from the 17th C. The imposing Hall, with its two-storeyed porch and fine mullioned windows, was built in 1641. Church House was once a church and school under a common roof. The inscription 'WF 1626' above the school door refers to its founder, William Fawcett, a wealthy wool merchant.

Three small **CAVE** entrances may be seen along the way. **WHARFESIDE CAVE** is a slit in a small cliff on the far side of the river. **YOCKENTHWAITE CAVE**, which discharges a stream, is on the L just before the stone circle. **HAGG BECK CAVE** is a fissure in a shallow gully a few yards to the R of the Horse Head path.

★

THE **STONE CIRCLE** PROBABLY DATES FROM THE BRONZE AGE (2000-500 BC). IT IS 25' IN DIAMETER AND IS REMARKABLY WELL PRESERVED.

The graceful bridge at Yockenthwaite

■ BECKERMONDS ■

is a tiny hamlet delectably situated on the Dales Way where the rushing waters of Oughtershaw Beck and Green Field Beck (*) eagerly unite to form the Wharfe. Refreshments *may* be available at East House Farm; at the time of writing (June 2000) the owner was considering catering for the needs of weary wayfarers.

East House Farm dates from 1760

✱ Green Field Beck is the one which flows under the *footbridge.*

HORSE HEAD PASS

an ancient route once trodden by monks, attains a height of 1952' at Horse Head Gate. The Rev. Thomas Lindley, incumbent of Halton Gill from 1807 until his 80th year in 1833, walked or rode over the pass on most Sundays – in all weathers – to conduct a service in Hubberholme Church.

The gates at the summit of Horse Head Pass. Ahead is a fine view of nearby Penyghent and distant Ingleborough.

THE WALKS - A PERSONAL RECORD

Nº	DATE	TIME Start	TIME Finish	NOTES (Weather, Companions, Highlights, Disasters etc.)	Marks out of 10
1					
2					
3					
4					
5					
6					
7					
8					
9					
10					
11					
12					
13					
14					
15					

WALKS IN DALES COUNTRY

AN ILLUSTRATED GUIDE TO
THIRTY SCENIC WALKS

JACK KEIGHLEY

GRINTON CHURCH, SWALEDALE   WALK II

2